Whom the Would Destroy,

or

How Not to Deregulate

Alfred E. Kahn
AEI–Brookings Joint Center
First Distinguished Lecture

AEI–Brookings Joint Center for Regulatory Studies

WASHINGTON, D.C.

2001

ISBN 0-8447-7156-2

1 3 5 7 9 10 8 6 4 2

The AEI Press
Publisher for the American Enterprise Institute
1150 17th Street, N.W.
Washington, D.C. 20036

Alfred E. Kahn

Contents

Foreword

This volume is the first in the Joint Center's Distinguished Lecture Series. The purpose of this series is to recognize individuals who have made outstanding contributions to the field of regulation. The honoree, who has complete latitude in selecting a topic for the lecture, is chosen by senior members of the Center on the basis of scholarly and practical contributions to the field.

The distinguished lecturer for 1999, Alfred E. Kahn, needs no introduction, so we will keep it short. In addition to having written the definitive two volumes on the economics of regulation, Fred has played a leading role in deregulating several U.S. industries, including the airlines, surface transportation, and telecommunications. He has also influenced economists and practitioners of the art of deregulation throughout the world. Fred is well known for his ability to explain abstract economic concepts—such as marginal cost pricing—in plain English.

We honor him for all his invaluable contributions.

ROBERT W. HAHN
ROBERT E. LITAN
AEI–Brookings Joint Center
for Regulatory Studies

1
Introduction

Having spent a major part of my career trying to draw a straight line from Marshall through Pigou and Abba Lerner to an elucidation and then application of the principles of economically efficient regulatorily prescribed pricing of public utility services, I am grateful for this opportunity to appraise the current status of the deregulation movement, in which I have likewise had the rare opportunity to play a leading role. In both those efforts, no one recognizes more clearly than I, my role was as nothing compared with the propelling forces of the double-digit inflations, "energy crises," and heightened environmental concerns of the middle and late 1970s—all of which suddenly emphasized the desirability of marginal cost pricing among the still-regulated "natural monopolies"[1] and of releasing the forces of competition among the airlines, in surface transportation, and in the energy sector.[2]

In this essay, I propose to concentrate on the continuation of the latter process in the revolutionary deregulation of much of the public utility industries over the past two decades, to which process I have devoted the major part of my attention during those years.[3] For the very reasons for which these industries were treated historically as public utilities, it has not been possible to subject them to the essentially flash-cut deregulation accorded transportation, oil, and gas. The consequent need, oxymoronically, for a regulated transition to "unregulation" has provided the occasion for pervasive demonstrations of the very propensities of regulation that are the principal reasons for its abandonment—propensities to micromanage the process; to prescribe the results that, it is anticipated, the Almighty would have produced if He or She were in full possession of the facts; to handicap the competitive process to produce visible competitors; and, opportunistically, to produce visible price reductions.

Since those tendencies were the subject of my hortatory *Letting Go* and presaged by my "Uneasy Marriage of Regulation and Competition,"[4] I will attempt here primarily to summarize the relevant portions of those previous expositions, then proceed to describe some more recent developments that I believe further illustrate those tendencies. In the process, I will explicitly confront the tension between Schumpeterian competition and the regulator's mandate to provide for the prompt dissolution of franchised monopoly; charges of opportunistic behavior on the part of both regulators and utility companies in the process of deregulation; and the jurisdictional question of what agency should be responsible for the necessarily continuing task of promoting and preserving efficient competition, with several recent, arresting illustrations of the pitfalls of that choice.

2

Telecommunications Deregulation: The Abominable TELRIC–BS

I begin with telecommunications, which continues most dramatically to exemplify the perverse propensities of regulatory agencies to micromanage the process—indeed to regulate pervasively in the name of "deregulation." The clearest example continues to be the Federal Communications Commission's prescription of what I take considerable pride in having christened the "blank-slate" version of total element long-run incremental costs (TELRIC–BS) as the basis for pricing the unbundled network elements (UNEs) that incumbent local exchange companies (ILECs) were required by the 1996 Telecommunications Act to make available to competitors.[5]

The Blank Slate

The FCC's proffered rationale for that prescription was that efficiency requires such prices be based neither on the average historical costs of building the network or network component nor on the marginal costs of the incumbent suppliers but instead on the marginal cost of replacing each element in a network embodying the best available current technology. I suppose that I should be flattered by the fact that the

Federal Communications Commission cited my *Economics of Regulation* six or seven times—and besides, who counts?—in its Notice of Proposed Rulemaking and then its Local Competition Order in general support of such pricing. I never dreamed, however, in proclaiming that efficient prices should be based on incremental costs, that policymakers would then proceed to ignore the *actual* incremental costs of the incumbent suppliers and instead adopt as the basis for policy the costs of a *hypothetical,* most efficient new entrant, constructing an entire set of facilities as though writing on a blank slate (with the one qualification that it take as given the existing wire center locations of the incumbents).

The entire logic of the marginal cost pricing principle requires that prices reflect the additional costs that society will actually incur or save if purchasers take somewhat more or somewhat less of the product or service in question. Prices set intentionally below that level by FCC decree, on the ground that the actual incremental costs of the ILECs doubtless reflect inefficiencies, clearly defeat that purpose; they induce buyers to demand (incremental) quantities of the services in question, the value of which to them is less than the (incremental) costs that society actually incurs in providing them.[6]

The blank-slate basis for marginal costing of individual network components ignores the fact that the most efficient or lowest marginal cost growth path for a firm with capacity already in existence will be constrained by the totality of its existing facilities; that will be true of each investment it makes henceforward in either additions to or replacements of existing facilities or equipment.[7] TELRIC–BS calculations for individual network elements—such as switches—that ignore the interrelatedness of cost-minimizing incremental decisions and the preexisting complements of facilities will tend systematically to understate actual incremental costs.

Because of the conceptual errors in the FCC's economic logic, the wide differences produced by its prescribed blank-slate models, consistently lower than the actual incremental cost estimates of the incumbent companies, are simply incredible and cannot be attributed to the natural tendency of regulators to underestimate and regulatees to exaggerate the costs on the basis of which rates are to be set. That *neither* party believes the blank-slate estimates is demonstrated by the fact that neither of them actually follows the logical implications, even though it would be the obligation of the former or in the clear interest of the latter to do so. If commissions that still regulate on a rate-base, rate-of-return basis believed those results, they would be derelict if they failed either to order the companies to scrap all their existing facilities forthwith and take the lower incremental cost route dictated by those models or disallow a large portion of their rate base on grounds of imprudence.[8] And in states that apply price caps, such results compel the conclusion that all the ILECs are run by idiots, who every day throw away dollars that they could otherwise pocket under a system of regulation that all of them advocated, precisely on the ground that it would give them undiluted incentives to minimize incremental costs—the only costs that *can* be minimized.

Most pertinent to my thesis here, the proclamation of the TELRIC–BS standard was an act of astounding *regulatory presumption*. While I do not myself dispute the need, in principle,[9] for a regulatory requirement that incumbent monopolists make their essential facilities available to competitors at prescribed reasonable prices, there are methods of doing so both procedurally and substantively inherently less thoroughly *regulatory* and correspondingly less *anticompetitive* than the path the FCC has taken. As for the price-setting mechanism, clearly if it is not to be traditional cost-of-service regulation, with its familiar deficiencies, then it should be rate caps such as have been introduced in the majority of states, which, while typically setting initial prices more or less on the basis of the current costs of the incumbent firms, then attempt to give to the regulated monopolists superior incentives to improve efficiency by divorcing the future course of those prices from their own costs, whether or not adding the goad of downward indexations for improvements in productivity estimated to be achievable on the basis of historical experience. The FCC's decision, instead, simply to prescribe at once what it thinks would be the outcome of that new form of incentive regulation flatly contradicts the reasoning that led both it and the majority of states to abandon cost-plus regulation and move to rate caps in the first place—namely, the inability of regulators to second-guess management decisions and evaluate those costs, except in cases of demonstrable imprudence, or to determine what the ultimate outcome of a competitive process would be.[10] And its open invitation to combat-by-engineering-and-econometric-models was eerily reminiscent of the constipation of the public utility regulatory process in the early decades of the past century by the controversies over the estimation of reproduction costs.[11]

Just as in rate-cap regulation, competitive markets set prices on the basis (roughly speaking) of the costs of incumbents. Those prices give challengers the proper target at which to shoot—the proper standard to meet or beat and the proper reward if they succeed. If they can achieve costs lower than that, firms will enter and in the process beat prices down to efficient levels. The FCC's choice, of—omnisciently—prescribing at once what it thinks would be the *outcome* of such a process, *short-circuits* it: why would competitors undertake the risks of major investments in their own facilities if they can lease them from the incumbent firms at what regulators speculate would be the minimum costs that an ideally efficient firm would incur constructing them afresh?

And yet I can think of no basis for questioning the general assumption, particularly in an industry with so dynamic a technology, that the most creative kind of competition is one in which rivals construct their own facilities rather than lease them from incumbents. As Justice Stephen Breyer has put it:

> Increased sharing by itself does not automatically mean increased competition. *It is in the unshared, not in the shared, portions of the enterprise that meaningful competition would likely emerge.* Rules that force firms to share every resource or element of a business would create, not competition, but pervasive regulation, for the regulators, not the marketplace, would set the relevant terms.[12]

The FCC and AT&T lawyers have dismissed the argument that the commission's TELRIC rule systematically discourages such facilities-based competition, on the ground that the competitive local exchange carriers (CLECs) have strong independent incentives to construct their own facilities, so as no longer to be dependent upon the ILECs. They might well have adduced, additionally, the many billions of dollars that the CLECs have indeed invested in their own facilities, particularly to serve large business customers in concentrated metropolitan areas—a history that Timothy J. Tardiff and I have summarized in a number of contexts.[13]

There are at least three rejoinders. First, the fact that the CLECs may indeed have such an incentive in no sense justifies the commission's offsetting or weakening it by making them in effect pay a price for that independence—the price of taking the risks of making the investments themselves and forgoing the opportunity to free ride by acquiring the network elements and the retail services from the ILECs at the lowest conceivable cost.

Second, the existing investments by the incumbents were massively encouraged by the distorted rate structures imposed upon the local telephone companies by their regulators—carrier access charges for the origination and completion of toll calls far in excess of costs, on the one side, and gross overcharges to business customers, particularly in those metropolitan areas, on the other—both to subsidize the underpricing of basic residential service. It is highly significant, therefore, that all the major CLECs—such as Teleport (since acquired by AT&T) and MFS (now part of MCI WorldCom)—began as independent providers of interexchange access, such as were present in every major metropolitan area before passage of the Telecommunications Act itself.

Third, as for the enormous expansion of those CLEC facilities in recent years, the investments have been preponderantly in high-speed, high-capacity fiberoptic facilities capable of offering new services such as Internet access, whereas the cost models employed to satisfy the FCC's prescription for pricing network elements typically assume that the ILEC would be providing facilities to handle narrowband, voice traffic. For example, for the shorter loops that one expects to find in urban areas, the models typically employ copper loops, whereas the CLECs are deploying fiber facilities, which have broadband capabilities.

The nature of those investments of the CLECs in a very interesting way undermines the entire logic of the TELRIC–BS prescription. By employing something like traditional prescribed rates of depreciation and return for the pricing of unbundled network elements, the FCC effectively assumes that the ILECs will for the most part remain monopoly suppliers of those components—an assumption clearly contradicted by its assertion about the preference of CLECs for using their own facilities. Moreover, as Tardiff has pointed out,[14] that asserted preference suggests a flat mismatch between the time perspective of the TELRIC–BS calculations and the intentions of the CLECs: many of the latter evidently regard the leasing of UNEs (or many of the UNEs) as only a short-term expedient. But in the presence of rapid technological change, that clearly means that the FCC's suggested traditional utility-type of return is wildly inappropriate. The cost of leasing a computer for a short period of time is typically much greater than the cost of purchasing one (assume that the purchase is on credit, to get comparable monthly or yearly costs), because the former throws the entire burden of obsolescence on the supplier.[15] The FCC's basis for dismissing concerns about the discouraging effect of its prescribed TELRIC–BS rates on the willingness and incentives of CLECs to construct their own facilities therefore flatly contradicts the assumptions underlying its pricing prescription, and in particular its failure to recognize that a true calculation of that cost would have to include gross rates of return far higher than have typically been prescribed by regulators and that the commission evidently contemplates itself.

The mirror image of the powerful temptation presented by TELRIC–BS prices for competitors to free ride on the facilities of the incumbents—all the greater in the presence of a highly dynamic technology—is that such prices discourage correspondingly risky investments by the incumbents, who are forced to share their facilities at those prescribed rates. As Robert W. Crandall has observed:

> [T]he modern telecommunications network is nothing like its counterpart of just 20 years ago. The local companies are constantly updating the networks to carry far more information at even-higher speeds. . . .
>
> Why should those firms invest in new, often risky technology for delivering advanced, high-speed services if they are to be required to offer any such new facilities to their rivals at cost?[16]

All of that is merely another way of saying that the FCC's decisions in 1996 through 1998 would have rated not an F but a zero from Joseph A. Schumpeter. TELRIC–BS, with its public utility gross rates of return, is essentially a construct of perfect competition; and perfect competition is in flat contradiction of the Schumpeterian preconditions of innovation—a truly startling deficiency, considering that the central purpose of the Telecommunications Act is to encourage the most rapid possible development of a modern telecommunications infrastructure. Manifestly, the greater the degree of innovation entailed by the investment, the greater the FCC's violation of Schumpeterian warnings in its combined prescription of mandatory sharing with competitors at TELRIC–BS prices.

That deplorable consequence of the TELRIC–BS prescription has thus far been partially concealed by the happenstance that the first issues in the *Iowa Utilities Board* case to reach the Supreme Court were the jurisdictional question of whether prescription of a method for costing and setting so-called default charges for network elements was properly within the authority of the FCC rather than the states, and whether the commission had gone beyond the criteria set down in the statute in prescribing the network elements subject to mandatory sharing. The pricing issue was specifically set aside and left for adjudication by the Eighth Circuit Court of Appeals,[17] which held, in July 2000, that while the FCC was entitled under the statute to base the prescribed prices of UNEs on the forward-looking—that is, incremental—costs of providing them (thereby ignoring historical or sunk costs), it violated "the plain meaning of the Act" when it based those charges on the costs of a hypothetical, most efficient carrier, constructing its network from scratch, rather than the actual costs that the ILECs would incur.[18]

Observe, for that reason, that Justice Breyer's abovementioned caveat to the FCC related only to mandated sharing (and not to the price prescribed by the FCC)—in a statement that deserves to be prominently displayed on the walls of every regulatory commission:

> Sharing requirements may diminish the original owner's incentive
> to keep up or to improve the property by depriving the owner of
> the fruits of the value-creating investment, research, or labor. . . .
> Nor can one guarantee that firms will undertake the investment
> necessary to produce complex technological innovations, know-
> ing that any competitive advantage deriving from those innova-
> tions will be dissipated by the sharing requirement.
>
> It is in the unshared, not in the shared, portion of the enter-
> prise that meaningful competition would likely emerge.[19]

There are some indications that the FCC has, at least in
part, come to see the error of its previous course. In its decision on the remand from the Supreme Court, the commission decided not to require the ILECs to share the
electronics required to provide digital subscriber line (DSL)
capability.[20]

The threat that the prescribed TELRIC–BS pricing of network elements posed to the recoverability of the incumbent
companies' heavy sunk costs, in the absence of any assurance by the FCC that they would be permitted to add a sufficient markup for that purpose, undoubtedly increased the
resistance of the ILECs to wholehearted cooperation in
opening their markets.[21] As I observe in chapter 5, I have
the strong impression that this experience contrasts sharply
with what was happening almost simultaneously in the
deregulation of the electric utilities, in the course of which
the Federal Energy Regulatory Commission at an early point
accepted the principle of stranded cost recovery.[22]

TELRIC–BS also opens up one final prospect so delicious
as to compel me, irresistibly, to repeat its exposition by
Dennis Weisman.[23] The place to begin is with the endorse-
ment of it as the basis for the mandated pricing of UNEs by
Professors William J. Baumol, Janusz A. Ordover, and
Robert D. Willig:

> TSLRIC [total service long-run incremental cost] is based on the
> costs an *efficient, cost-minimizing* competitor would incur—i.e., the
> costs of assets that are optimally configured and sized with current

technology and efficient operating practices. Proper TSLRIC estimates do not simply accept the architecture, sizing, technology, or operating decisions of the ILECs as bases for calculating TSLRIC.[24]

Baumol has been a leading, persuasive proponent of incumbent regulated companies' being permitted to price down to incremental costs—*their own* incremental costs, he has emphasized—in competitive situations.[25] The prospect, then, is that an ILEC might well be prohibited from meeting the lower price of a CLEC *using the ILEC's own network components:* one can readily imagine the scorn with which the incumbent would be greeted if it demanded the right to price below its own LRIC to meet the competition of rivals using its own facilities, purchased at rates deliberately set, in accordance with the foregoing Baumol prescription, at the LRIC of "an efficient, cost-minimizing competitor," rather than—as the competitors will undoubtedly insist—at costs grounded in "the architecture, sizing, technology, [and] operating decisions of the ILEC" itself!

Defining the "Increment" as the Total Service

My criticisms of the FCC's prescription for the pricing of UNEs have heretofore applied only to the blank-slate aspect: I have seen no similar objection to its total element component—that is to say, to its taking on the aspect of *average total* incremental cost. The justification, I presume, would be that if there are economies of scale in the provision of some of those elements, such that the average cost of smaller increments is less that of the entire service, competitive parity between incumbents and challengers calls for no discrimination between them in the (average incremental) costs they bear.

That assumption might seem to conflict with the logic of my consistent criticism of the FCC's employment of blank-slate costs—namely, that efficient competition must be conducted on the basis of the respective *actual* LRICs of the several rivals, which would, in the presence of economies of scale, be below TSLRIC. In those circumstances, the choice between the two pricing principles as the basis of charges to competitors would come down—as so many of the regulatory issues in utility industries in process of deregulation seem to have an inexorable tendency to do—to a question of how *total* costs (or revenue entitlement) may most efficiently be recovered, consistently with efficient competition. The FCC's reasoning—implicit, it appears—may have been that just as it recognized that charges for network elements based on TELRIC would in principle properly have added to them a contribution to the recovery of common costs, so basing them on the LRIC that the incumbents actually confronted would require adding a markup, correspondingly, to recover the difference between the total service and the simple long-run incremental cost.[26] In addition, the commission's reasoning may have been that so long as that markup above LRIC in the charges to competitors was incorporated also in the ILECs' retail prices of the services employing those inputs, competitive parity would be preserved (that is, the efficient component pricing rule respected).[27]

I have previously taken issue with the FCC's adoption of the total service measure of (average) incremental cost as the basis for its prescribed wholesale discounts on ILEC sales to resellers.[28] Since the identical issue has arisen in the deregulation of retail electricity markets, with some state regulatory commissions (and not others) committing the same error, I postpone to my discussion below of electricity "shopping credits" my identical criticisms of the FCC's application of the total service increment and explain why wholesale discounts equated to long-run incremental cost instead would be a necessary condition of efficient competition.

On the other hand, the decision of the commission in December 1999 not to prescribe TSLRIC–BS pricing in its positive response to the demands of CLECs for "line" or "spectrum sharing" seems to have been deliberately—and correctly—intended to put entrants and incumbents alike on the same competitive plane.[29] In that proceeding the FCC acceded to the request of some applicant carriers that the ILECs be required to offer the use of the high-frequency portion of the spectrum provided by their subscriber loops, for carriage of digital signals to packet switches. Setting aside the question whether the commission should have added that new "network element" to its list for mandatory sharing at all—a subject to which I return—the logic of its decision was plausible: a CLEC interested in competing only for the business of transmitting massive volumes of data at high speed does not require the entire loop. All that is arguably "necessary," lack of access to which would "impair" its ability to offer that service,[30] is access to the high-frequency portion of the spectrum, leaving the lower frequencies for transmission of analog voice signals via the circuit-switched network.

Had the FCC applied its TELRIC prescription to that separate network element, it would presumably have required a price close to zero. That is the result that would be produced by the now-familiar method of measuring the TSLRICs of products supplied in common. As the FCC explicitly recognized in its decision, the incremental cost of common service B is the difference between the cost of providing its common product A on a stand-alone basis and the cost of providing A and B together. If, then, a loop is conceived—as the FCC did—as making it possible to supply two services (transmission of voice and high-speed-high-capacity transmission of data), the TSLRIC of *either of them* would turn out to be close to zero if not actually zero, since any system set up to supply the other would already have incorporated the costs of the loop itself.[31]

A prescribed zero price for high-frequency access would not in itself have violated the requirements of efficient competition between incumbents and challengers. Presumably, the incremental cost of that new use of the loop is or would be something close to zero for incumbents as well, so that a similar availability of that portion of it to their competitors at similarly low-to-zero marginal cost would put them on an even competitive footing. The ILECs argued, however, as did I,[32] that if an incumbent local telephone company is to be required to bear the entire cost of providing a loop capable of providing a wide variety of services—with the necessity of recovering a portion of its costs in higher-than-competitive charges for those several services rather than (as efficiency would dictate) in a lump-sum charge for dial tone alone[33]—and is then required to offer the access that the loop provides to competitors for the provision of only some of those services at zero incremental cost, it may well find itself, under pressure of competition, incapable of recovering any of the common costs from the latter services. Competitive parity, they contended—following the same logic as I have just expounded for pricing UNEs at TSLRIC rather than at LRIC in the presence of economies of scale or scope—would therefore require that both sets of rivals bear the same loop costs—not that one set of rivals be totally exempted from them.

Evidently deferring to those last protests, the FCC departed from its previously proclaimed and putatively inviolable blank-slate total element long-run incremental cost standard in pricing that new element (which presumably would have produced a zero price) and required merely that the ILECs charge their competitors for it whatever they allocated to their own asymmetric digital subscriber line (ADSL) services.[34] Observe that such a standard preserves comparative parity, while not interfering with the ability of the ILEC to recover the costs of the loop,[35] since it recovers as large a contribution to its total costs in its charges to CLECs as it would recover if it provided those data services in the same way itself. As the commission points out, the ILECs are already recovering the full embedded costs of their loops, and nothing in its present decision detracts from that recovery.[36] But observe also that its reasoning and solution here do represent a laudable implicit abandonment of the logic of TELRIC–BS—a small forward step for mankind.

3

To Share or Not to Share: Schumpeter and Deregulation Revisited

The local telephone companies—and electric distribution companies, as well, in a similar situation—have, unsurprisingly, taken the position generally that the obligation to share should be confined to essential facilities, strictly defined.[37] For that view, they have ample precedent under the antitrust laws, to the effect that "there is no general duty to share. Compulsory access, if it exists at all, is and should be very exceptional."[38]

According to that standard, the requisite conditions would be that the input in question be essential to the production or supply of a competitive service, available only from a monopolist that also competes in the offering of the latter service, and incapable of being economically duplicated by others. Outstanding examples of such facilities in the electric utility business are, of course, the transmission and distribution lines of the incumbent, vertically integrated companies (except where—and until—on-site generation is economically feasible). Ensuring access to these facilities on nondiscriminatory terms by all competing generators and marketers is an essential component of all plans for exposing the latter functions to competition.

There are strong reasons in unregulated industries for *not* requiring competitors to share with their rivals inputs that do not satisfy the criteria of essentiality, thus strictly defined. The essence of competition is the attempt to develop just such advantages; to require their sharing in instances in which that quest has been successful would therefore discourage competition itself. That is the logic of Judge Hand's famous and, to my knowledge, universally accepted, warning, in his *Alcoa* decision, "that the successful competitor, having been urged to compete, must not be turned upon when he wins."[39] In view of the fact that competition and innovation themselves consist of a quest for differential advantage, a requirement that the benefits be shared, on regulatorily dictated terms, in the cases in which that quest has been successful would interfere with the competitive process itself—the greater the risks involved in that quest, the greater the interference with Schumpeterian innovation.

I have myself argued, however—and express some satisfaction that I have persuaded several electric distribution companies to accept the proposition—that a reasonable case can be made in the context of the introduction of competition into public utility industries that typically an incumbent company not only will control some facilities truly "essential" to its rivals but also will enjoy economies of scale or scope not because of superior enterprise on its part but merely because of its inherited franchised monopoly, and that requiring it to share the benefit of those facilities with rivals at a compensatory price would therefore not entail penalizing successful competitive efforts.[40]

Such a softening of the essential facilities doctrine in the public utility context—the legitimacy of which seems to me in principle unexceptionable—might well be so difficult to administer as to be impractical, except in a few specific contexts.[41] Any such required sharing would have to be qualified by a stipulation that the obligation would apply only to the extent feasible and that the charges for such inputs—materials, goods, or services—reflect any additional costs of making them available to those outsiders. As Ronald Coase and Oliver E. Williamson have pointed out, the reason businesses integrate—that is, conduct a number of operations under the umbrella of a single financially affiliated entity, rather than through market transactions—is, in a fundamental sense, the belief that subjection of those several operations to unitary managerial control permits the achievement of savings of transactions costs and avoids the uncertainties of trying to achieve the requisite coordination by purchases and sales in the market.[42] In those circumstances, the notion of requiring a firm to share economies "equally" with its own affiliated operations and outsiders contradicts the essential nature of a firm. What would it mean to require a utility company—if it is to share with unregulated affiliates computing facilities, procurement, office space, service vehicles, or experience in offering both regulated distribution of electric power and the unregulated energy itself (along with similarly unregulated energy-related services) in the competitive market—to "share" them also with outsiders? If it tried to sell some portion of those "shared resources" to nonaffiliates, the transactions cost of doing so could well eat up the difference between the incremental cost of providing them and their market value. If that were not so, there would be no point in conducting those several operations instead within the firm. These economies are likely to be specific to the integrated nature of the utility company and its affiliate. We rarely see firms in competitive markets renting out employees or equipment or experience to others for short periods of time. But the principle I would support remains: the sharing obligation should apply where the economies flow simply from the incumbent company's status as a franchised monopoly, to the extent sharing is practicable.

Such a requirement of course invites disagreements—for example, about what collaborations are or are not "practicable"—and complaints, just as there may well be disagreements over whether electric utility companies are fully complying with their obligation to provide equal access to such unexceptionably essential facilities as transmission and distribution lines or competitively sensitive customer information, and just as there are and will undoubtedly continue to be intense disagreements about whether the local Bell companies are complying with the 1996 Telecommunications Act's long checklist in section 271 of the ways in which they are obliged to open their local markets to competitors as a precondition for relief from the ban on their offering service between local access and transport areas (LATAs). To resolve such disputes, regulatory commissions are finding or are likely to find it desirable to institute informal resolution procedures, conducted either directly by them or under their auspices.[43]

Indeed, the 1996 act clearly contemplated just such a process for identifying the unbundled network elements to be shared and setting the terms on which they were to be made available to competitors. The competitors must first request access; the ILECs are then obliged to negotiate in good faith, and in the event of a failure to agree, either party can petition the state commission to conduct binding arbitrations of disputed issues. In either event, the terms are to be approved, disapproved, or prescribed by the commission—all within ten months of the original request for negotiations. It was this process that the FCC short-circuited—no doubt with the intention of facilitating it—by stipulating the elements that were to be made available, prescribing the method by which the prices were to be determined, and establishing "default" TSLRIC–BS prices for the commissions to apply. The FCC's intervention was overturned by the Eighth Circuit on the ground that it departed from that statutorily prescribed process and vesting of at least initial authority in the state commissions but was sustained by the Supreme Court majority as within the FCC's legal authority—to the vigorous (and, I must confess, to me entirely persuasive) dissents of Justices Stephen Breyer and Clarence Thomas.

I am not able to judge whether what I see as the procedure specified by the statute would have been more successful. States such as Texas and California have used "workshops" as part of the section 251 and 271 processes; on the basis of my limited exposure to such proceedings, I could hardly describe them as models of expedition. It seems to me at least possible, however, that this was the fault of the ridiculous pricing standard that the FCC specified—an open invitation to blue-sky as well as blank-slate model building.[44] On the other hand, the U.S. Telephone Association reported that as of December 1998 the process had produced some 6,000 interconnection agreements, and, as I have already observed, local competition is progressing vigorously in service to businesses in concentrated metropolitan areas.[45]

Curtis Grimm and Clifford Winston have presented what seems to me an important and extremely persuasive case for just such voluntary collaborations to increase the opportunities for competition in the now highly concentrated railroad industry—and correspondingly offering captive shippers the opportunity to invoke its benefits—in the widespread situations in which the shippers depend for part of their service on a single bottleneck railroad.[46] Such arrangements as reciprocal switching or exchanges of trackage rights by carriers in control of bottleneck facilities and the constitution of jointly owned, independently managed terminal-switching railroads with a mandate to provide equal access to the partners are already widespread, no doubt because they typically involve reciprocal exchanges of benefits. Others have been adopted by merging parties, either as an explicit condition imposed by the regulatory authorities or quasi-voluntarily, as in the case of Norfolk Southern and CSX, to make their proposed acquisition of Conrail more palatable to shippers and to the Surface Transportation Board and because they could not agree which of the two would end up in control of important markets. Under the Grimm-Winston proposal the railroads would be further pressed to adopt such arrangements by the transfer of authority over mergers from the complaisant STB to the Department of Justice, but the railroads would be encouraged also by the offer of full deregulation in exchange.

The sharing requirement for public utilities that I have proposed—somewhat more liberal than would be prescribed for unregulated industries generally under the essential facilities doctrine—must not be permitted to obscure the fundamental propositions to which it provides the exception. First, it justifies mandatory sharing only of facilities or capabilities carried over from the public utility past. Second, wherever mandatory sharing, for the sake of jump-starting the entry of competitors, would interfere with the more creative and dynamic investment in facilities-based competitive entry and innovation by incumbents and challengers alike, it is the latter that must take primacy.

Tested against those principles, the FCC's Local Competition Order in 1996, requiring the ILECs to provide competitors with all network elements to which access is technically feasible, clearly deserved the rebuke that it received from the Supreme Court. If rivals can share whatever ILEC facilities they ask for that can feasibly be provided, at TSLRIC–BS prices—with their mere asking satisfying the conditions for mandatory sharing set forth in the Telecommunications Act—it cannot but have a discouraging effect on their own initiative and innovation. As Jerry

A. Hausman and J. Gregory Sidak have incisively observed,[47] the lower the FCC–mandated charge for UNEs—the less it allows for the risks of innovation and obsolescence—the more that element will inevitably satisfy the test of "essentiality," namely, that it be unobtainable from other sources and uneconomic to duplicate.

When we consider the line- or spectrum-sharing decision in isolation, the logic of the FCC's requiring the ILECs to make their copper wires available to competitors for this purpose is readily comprehensible and, at least at first blush, not inconsistent with Schumpeterian considerations: to the extent that that basic network element provides the competitive advantage of low-cost access to the high-frequency spectrum, it is an advantage that accrues to the incumbents not from superior enterprise, efficiency, or innovation, but as the mere consequence of their inherited local franchised monopolies. Following the logic that I have already expounded, there would seem to be no loss to competition in requiring the ILECs to share that advantage with others, and doing so would facilitate competitive entry.

And yet, it is also impossible to dismiss a concern that the FCC has been overly eager to graft rules designed to create opportunities for competitive entry into basic telephone service, in which the incumbent monopolists are conceived of as controlling the sine qua non of entry, onto a situation so dynamic, technologically and commercially, that the model contemplated by the Telecommunications Act in 1996 simply does not apply:

> it is impossible to argue that one company holds or is ever likely to hold monopoly control. . . . Today, there are hundreds of companies competing to offer high-speed Internet access using four principal technologies—cable, satellite, wireless transmission, and digital subscriber lines, or DSL, delivered over existing telephone lines.[48]

It seems especially anomalous for the commission to have imposed the sharing obligation on the ILECs, which are markedly behind their major competitors, the cable companies, and spending billions of dollars a year in an attempt to catch up—a race accelerated by hundred-billion-dollar investments by AT&T, in acquiring TCI and MediaOne, and AOL's merger with Time Warner; and in which, finally, the overwhelming primacy of preserving Schumpeterian incentives must make one highly skeptical of the FCC's attempt to redress what it sees as one imbalance by extending the terms of the Telecommunications Act, however plausibly, to one group of competitors alone.

For all those reasons, the commission decided—correctly—in its preliminary decision in the Supreme Court remand proceedings, not to require the ILECs to share with competitors the electronics required to provide DSL capability: its line-sharing decision relates only to the high-frequency capabilities of the subscriber loop itself (which can evidently be split off with a relatively simple device). The possibility remains, however, that such a requirement impedes or discourages them from upgrading their entire networks—for example, by more widespread installation of fiber.[49]

4

The InterLATA Prohibition and High-Speed Data Transmission

My own involvements in the most recent controversies over mandated sharing of access to high-speed, high-capacity transmission facilities have been limited—in part because, as my foregoing comments about the spectrum-sharing issue will doubtless have demonstrated, I have only something like an early nineteenth-century grasp of the technologies involved. A closely related regulatory issue to which I have given considerable attention, however, has been raised by the regional Bell operating companies' (RBOCs') petition for relief from interLATA restrictions insofar as they apply to their building and operating advanced broadband data networks—relief provided in the bill introduced in the 107th Congress by Representatives W. J. Tauzin and John D. Dingell, H.R. 1542.

That effort of the RBOCs—limited as it is to high-speed transmission of data, including Internet access—is in a sense opportunistic, since they would, of course, like to be free of the current constraint entirely. I have supported that broader effort in testimony submitted in section 271 proceedings jointly with Timothy Tardiff on two grounds: the undeniable benefits of the additional competition that the RBOCs would bring to interLATA markets, on the one side,[50] and the proposition, equally undeniable, that the original, historical purpose of the interLATA prohibition—emergence of a competitive long-distance market independent of the local company monopolies and incapable of being remonopolized by them—has been fully and irreversibly achieved.

In taking that position, we have necessarily recognized that the 1996 act, in a sense likewise opportunistically, grafted a second purpose onto the continuation of the prohibition—namely, by withholding the lifting of the ban until the RBOCs had cooperated sufficiently in opening their local markets, to encourage local competition both as an end in itself and as a means of eliminating the danger of ILECs' using local monopoly power to impair competition in other markets.[51]

In opposing every single one of the RBOC applications for removal of the interLATA ban—including the one (by Bell Atlantic for New York) approved by the FCC[52]—before capitulating to the Southwestern Bell application for Texas, the Department of Justice displayed a single-minded dedication to the second purpose of maximizing the opportunities for local competition. Paradoxically, however—considering that the whole purpose of the AT&T divestiture and the associated interLATA prohibition was to substitute structural solutions for injunctive remedies (which would have had to be policed)—both the Department of Justice and the FCC have, in so doing, displayed also a greater commitment to regulatory enforcement than the Telecommunications Act itself envisions. On the other hand, both those agencies might be entitled to point to the ultimate success of the Bell Atlantic application—and, in June 2000, that of SWB for Texas—as a vindication of their insistence on the thoroughgoing and extremely expensive compliance efforts of both the company and the New York—and Texas—commissions and the thoroughly regulatory enforcement arrangements instituted by them.

Of course, the Telecommunications Act does require the RBOCs to meet a series of conditions (fourteen to be precise) before the FCC can lift the interLATA entry restriction. Yet, rather than require regulators merely to satisfy themselves that those "requisite *arrangements* necessary to open the local market are *made available*"[53] in that fashion, the Department of Justice, primarily through two affidavits submitted on its behalf by Professor Marius Schwartz, consistently urged the FCC additionally to assess the degree to which that availability had actually proved *effective*—that is, to determine whether local markets had been "irreversibly opened to competition" by looking to see whether "meaningful local competition" had in fact emerged.[54] Where sufficient competition had not taken root, Professor Schwartz would have had the Justice Department impose on the RBOCs responsibility for rebutting the presumption that their actions had been responsible for that failure—precisely the complicated and controversial issues that the law presumably intended to head off by simply requiring RBOC applicants to satisfy a checklist of specific actions and arrangements necessary to *permit* competitive entry.[55] That is to say, while the law requires the RBOCs to open the door, the Antitrust Division would have retained the sanction if competitors had not actually walked through, unless the incumbents could prove that it was not their fault.

In view of the clashing interests of the RBOCs and would-be local competitors in negotiating the terms of entry, the incentive of the long-distance companies and their CLEC affiliates to quarrel over those terms to delay the RBOCs' entry into competition with them, and the regulatorily distorted rate structures that in any event discourage competitive entry into local residential and rural markets, the proposals of the Justice Department would seem to be a recipe for pervasive litigation and regulation as far as the eye can see.

To its credit, the FCC rejected that invitation in the Bell Atlantic case and confined its attention to insisting on a strict satisfaction of the fourteen-point checklist.

Whatever the balance of pros and cons of lifting the interLATA prohibition generally, the question raised by the Tauzin-Dingell bill is whether there are reasons specific to data that would tilt the balance further toward its removal for that traffic. It seems to me that there are. Whatever residual danger there is of the RBOCs' using their control over access to ultimate subscribers to impede long-distance competition in the case of voice messages, that danger is somewhere in the range between enormously reduced and negligible in the case of high-speed Internet access. Any provider of long-distance services generally must be able to reach every phone in the country, for the most part via the incumbent local exchange carrier. As Douglas B. Bernheim and Robert D. Willig have pointed out, that exposes a subscriber who chooses to bypass an ILEC at the originating end to the continued possibility of discriminatory treatment at the terminating end.[56] In the case of high-speed Internet service, in contrast, all a competitive carrier needs to do is reach an Internet service provider; and those, I understand, have points of presence, if not universally, then in LATAs with the overwhelming bulk of traffic. It is not necessary for the messages to pass through the facilities of the ILEC at the destination end.

As for uses of packet switching other than Internet access, the recipients at the destination end will, in contrast with voice messages, typically be either affiliates of the sender or other large businesses, fully capable in most cases of bypassing ILECs. That circumstance thereby largely removes the impediment to competition identified by Bernheim and Willig.

Since most Internet access messages do not have to cross LATA boundaries, it might appear that the RBOCs need no relief from the interLATA prohibition to provide that service. What the restriction does, however, is handicap them in their attempts to serve customers in the most efficient way possible and by so doing limits the customers for whose patronage they can economically compete. It does so by preventing the commingling of Internet access, which they can offer the overwhelming majority of customers without crossing LATA boundaries, with other high-speed data transmission services—from one particular subscriber to another particular destination—that do have, explicitly, to cross those boundaries. Furthermore, the restriction prohibits the provision of both those forms of service *with the most efficient configuration of facilities.* As a result, the RBOCs are forced to build redundant facilities within each LATA, to handle the intraLATA business that they are free to solicit, instead of the integrated regional facilities that would have been best adapted to provide intra- and interLATA service together.

Further—and in a real sense definitively—the RBOCs do not possess in the provision of high-capacity services the kind of original monopoly that they had in voice service, or such monopoly as may be inferred from the fact that they continue to be the local service provider for the overwhelming majority of subscribers in their franchise territories. On the contrary, *they are markedly behind the cable companies.*[57] So the essential premise of the prohibition, so far as concerns the high-speed transmission of data, is simply not valid. If the danger of use of a predominant position in the provision of access were to justify prohibitions on participation in the markets that make use of that input, there would be a much stronger case for prohibiting AT&T, TCI, MediaOne, or other cable companies from the right to transmit data interLATA—which I emphatically do not recommend—than for continuing the prohibition on the RBOCs.

If, in such circumstances, there are even more compelling positive reasons to lift the ban for data than in the case of voice, it becomes possible—if not, indeed, mandatory—to conclude that the goals of our national telecommunications policy will be more fully and quickly achieved by a lifting of the interLATA prohibition, so far as the transmission of data is concerned, even though it involves some diminution in the attractiveness of the carrot that the FCC is using to induce the RBOCs to cooperate in opening their local markets.

The positive reasons are that Schumpeterian considerations appear to apply to the data transmission market with unusual force. First, data traffic is growing much more rapidly than voice. Second, the ILECs are constructing packet-switched networks especially suited to handle this rapidly growing demand—facilities not yet fully suitable for voice transmission, because they do not yet produce signals of sufficient quality. Third, the provision of high-speed Internet access, the universal availability of which has become of major concern nationally, requires the high-capacity access that the telephone companies can most efficiently provide only by very large, risky investments in digitalizing their access lines, in competition with other suppliers using other technologies. Finally, the interLATA prohibition artificially handicaps the RBOCs in that competition both by limiting the traffic they are permitted to carry and by inflating their costs of carrying it.

5

Stranded Costs and Regulatory Opportunism

I have thus far studiously avoided even alluding to perhaps the most contentious issue associated with deregulation, doubtless because it has involved the largest number of visible dollars—the question of the entitlement of utility companies to recover sunk costs threatened with being "stranded" under pressure of competition. Part of the reason for that forbearance is that I have fully laid out my views on this subject elsewhere.[58] Another part is that the issue is inherently a political one, although one cannot ignore its economic implications—the violation of allocative efficiency that stranded cost recovery entails, on the one side, and, on the other, the unmeasurable effect on future investment incentives of opportunistic behavior on the part of government (the latter doubtless diluted by the notoriously short memories of investors and the virtual uniqueness of the issue). As I pointed out in 1985, after maintaining that in principle electric companies were entitled to recover such costs of construction of nuclear plants as could not be found to have been imprudently incurred:

> [N]o social or institutional arrangement can possibly be followed blindly, without any exercise of judgment, in the face of all contingencies, no matter how extreme. The abandonment, or even the entry into service, of multibillion-dollar plants is an event so extraordinary in its consequences that it would be unreasonable to

insist on a blind allegiance to a contract that could not possibly have contemplated such an extreme contingency.

In these circumstances, spreading the burden fairly between investors and ratepayers involves two kinds of judgments: First, an economic judgment—a balancing of the immediate benefits to ratepayers of putting the major burden on the company against the higher costs they will in that event have to bear in the future, if whatever company serves them is to attract capital and provide good service; and, second, a political judgment, in the best sense of that term, of what settlement would be the fairest.[59]

In light of that conception of the stranded cost issue, while I have no difficulty accepting Paul L. Joskow's characterization of regulatory commissions' demanding immediate rate reductions as a price for such settlements as "opportunistic," I would add that linking recovery by the companies of the major portion of the cost of investments that turned out very badly with rate reductions may well also have constituted a fair settlement.[60]

Moreover, it appears that the early acceptance by FERC and the several state commissions of the principle of stranded cost recovery via markups in the regulated charges for transmission and distribution—with those same markups recovered also in the wholesale and retail prices of the incumbent utility companies, thereby ensuring competitive parity[61]—helped to elicit the cooperation of the incumbent utility companies in ensuring access of competitive generators and marketers to those essential facilities.[62] As I have already suggested, the failure of the FCC to offer any such convincing assurance to the telephone companies can have had only the opposite effect on their cooperativeness in opening their local markets and may well prove therefore to have been short-sightedly opportunistic.

Much more blatantly opportunistic has been the policy of some regulatory commissions of requiring that when assets are transferred from utility companies to unregulated affiliates, they be transferred at market or book value, whichever is higher. When the market value of a utility company's plant is less than its book value—a demonstration that commission-allowed depreciation recoveries to date have fallen short of economic levels—the firm is in principle entitled to recover the difference—the costs that would be stranded by competition—from ratepayers. Conversely, if the firm transfers or sells plant whose market value exceeds book—reflective, by definition, of depreciation overrecoveries—the difference belongs to those ratepayers. The policy of the commissions to which I have alluded, in contrast, amounts to "tails you lose" (in the former situation), "heads we win" (in the latter). Needless to say, regulators are not the only ones who play this game: unsurprisingly, in consideration of my own virtuous consistency, I have been hired only by companies confronted with deregulation that find themselves in the former situation.[63]

At the same time, the fact that all of the deregulatory action appears to be in the former situations—confronting commissions with a bill for the deficiencies in past depreciation rates—rather than the latter—offering them the opportunity to demand refunds to ratepayers of their previous overpayments of depreciation—does not constitute grounds for legitimate ratepayer complaint, although at least one asserted representative of their interests has lodged it. As Paul L. Joskow has documented, the deregulation movement in electric power, understandably, has concentrated on the jurisdictions in which competition promised to reduce rates below regulated levels reflecting historical or book costs, thus threatening to strand some of those costs.[65] Not surprisingly, consumers generally have been content to stick with regulation in the opposite circumstance, in which book costs produced rates below competitive levels.[65] As I once wrote to another former regulator who had complained about the apparently larger number of cases in which expert witnesses had appeared on behalf of utility companies in support of the recoverability of stranded costs than where the competitive market value of assets exceeded net book value, the *political process*—specifically, the geographical selectivity of the movement toward deregulation—has been the visible hand that redressed the balance. I had it on good authority, I assured him, that Adam Smith was smiling in his grave.

6

Preserving—and Distorting—Competition

The more troublesome manifestations of regulatory opportunism, to an economist, are to be found in the efforts of commissions purportedly aimed at ensuring that the competition ushered in by deregulation is fair and efficient.

Deregulation assumes the superiority of competition and therefore increases the importance of policies aimed at preserving and promoting it. That is axiomatic. What is far from axiomatic is how best that purpose can be achieved and what agencies should be entrusted with the responsibility for ensuring its achievement. I find extremely troublesome the tendency of commissions to display signs of regulatory opportunism in fulfilling that responsibility.

The Jurisdictional Issue

The predilection of most economists is to entrust the responsibility for managing the transition from regulation to deregulation to the antitrust authorities, with their presumed superior expertise in comprehending the requirements of effective competition, rather than to the former regulatory agencies, particularly because of the demonstrated proclivities of those agencies to protectionism and cartelization, including a tendency to condemn any and all price-cutting as "predatory" or "destructive."[66] Closely related are the tendencies of regulators to seize opportunities to produce reductions in the rates for still-regulated services and visible *competitors*, at the expense of *competition,* in the unregulated markets[67]—for example, by exacting "royalties" from utility companies' unregulated operations, or ransom payments for employees transferred from regulated to unregulated operations or by otherwise hamstringing the utility companies in the exploitation of economies of scale and scope in the latter markets.[68]

At the same time—despite those systemic transgressions—I cannot yet bring myself to deny the regulatory agencies a central role in the transition of public utilities to competition, in view of the special circumstances of those industries: the necessity for settling out and tracking the collection of strandable costs; the more pervasive possibilities in those industries of tying competitive to monopoly services, directly or subtly, and of cross-subsidization, strictly defined; the consequent need for accounting separations and the monitoring of transactions between still-regulated utilities and unregulated affiliates; and, finally, the pervasiveness of essential facilities controlled by incumbents— not to mention competitive advantages deriving solely from their historical franchised monopolies, requiring an administrative agency to define them and to prescribe the terms and conditions of sharing.[69] The foregoing circumstances of formerly comprehensively regulated industries by no means exclude the antitrust authorities from playing a—or, indeed, the—major role in preserving competition during the transition to deregulation; they do seem to me, however, reasons why the regulators have an important role to play as well— in compliance with the principles of efficient competition.

A Digression on Assertedly Predatory Airline Pricing. In view of my recognition of the several reasons for entrusting the preservation of competition in industries in the process of deregulation to the antitrust agencies rather than to regulatory commissions, I feel compelled to defend the prominent role I have played in supporting the initiative of the U.S. Department of Transportation to exercise its independent statutory authority to proscribe "exclusionary practices" in the airline industry.[70] Since I have defended that position at length elsewhere[71] and played a role in marshaling and articulating it in the recent report of the Transportation Research Board/National Research Council on the airline industry,[72] I confine myself here to the briefest possible reconciliation of those two positions.[73]

The critical elements in that reconciliation are that the airline industry has proved to be far more susceptible to highly discriminatory pricing than most proponents of deregulation envisioned[74] and to predatory defenses of those price structures; and that the latter practices ought in principle to be more subject to successful attack under the proscription of "exclusionary practices" under the separate authority of the DOT—the counterpart of the authority of the Federal Trade Commission to act against unfair methods of competition in industry generally—than under the Sherman Act, as it has been interpreted in the past several years.

The major explanations of the first of these phenomena—in addition to what have proved to be very large economies of scale and scope—are that, first, the preponderant number of city-pair markets are served by only one or two carriers; second, airline routes are not as contestable as most proponents of deregulation had claimed or hoped; and third, therefore, potential entry cannot be relied upon to protect travelers fully on such routes.[75] In such imperfect markets, the major carriers have become extremely sophisticated in practicing price discrimination, which has produced an enormously increased spread between discounted and average fares, on the one side, and full fares, on the other. While that development is almost certainly welfare-enhancing, on balance, it also raises the possibility of monopolistic exploitation of demand-inelastic travelers.

In such circumstances, experience has demonstrated, it is of disproportionately great importance that the pricing of the major carriers be disciplined by the potential entry of low-cost, more or less uniformly low-fare-charging carriers—in effect (when successful) imposing the economically proper ceiling of stand-alone costs.[76]

The airline industry is, however, especially susceptible to predatory responses to such entry because of the mobility of aircraft: the incumbents need incur virtually no additional sunk costs when they increase capacity on challenged routes, while new entrants can be readily induced to depart because of their ability correspondingly to move their equipment out.[77] In addition, the extreme sophistication of the yield-management practices of the major airlines enables them also to increase sharply the availability of deeply discounted fares on individual routes in response to competitive challenge and to withdraw them when the challenge disappears.[78]

For all the foregoing reasons, the principal component of the average variable (or short-run marginal) cost floor of nonpredatory pricing prescribed by the Areeda-Turner test clearly is or should be variable *opportunity* cost—the revenue forgone elsewhere by transferring capacity to the contested route or the revenue from undiscounted or only modestly discounted ticket sales sacrificed by the suddenly increased availability of deeply discounted ones or both—rather than *production* cost. That is the essence of the condition incorporated in all three indicators of "unfair exclusionary practices" proposed by the Department of Transportation: that "the ensuing self-diversion of revenue results in lower local revenue than would a reasonable alternative response."[79]

I have little confidence, however, that the courts will accept this definition of predatory pricing under the antitrust laws: the present majority on the Supreme Court has, under the lingering influence of the University of Chicago, virtually written predation out of the antitrust laws—at a time when, ironically, the consensus of academic economic opinion has moved to a "post–University of Chicago" position on the subject—a move from which I, as a premature post-Chicagoan of several decades' standing, take particular satisfaction.[80]

In such circumstances, I am unwilling to surrender the alternative authority of the Department of Transportation to proceed against unfairly exclusionary practices. It is highly ironic that some opponents of its initiative, which has been—just as was deregulation itself—violently opposed by virtually the entire incumbent industry and supported by representatives of airline travelers and consumers generally, should cite in support of their opposition the tendency of administrative agencies generally to be excessively responsive to and protective of the industries under their jurisdiction![81]

An Illustration of the Comparative Propensities of the Antitrust Agencies and a Regulatory Agency to Meddle. I have already pointed to the tendency of the Department of Justice, in section 271 telecommunications matters, to impose conditions that pose the threat of introducing excessively intrusive regulation into what was intended to be a process of deregulation. That transgression by the department was dwarfed by the transgressions of the FCC in treating the proposed merger of Southwestern Bell and Ameritech, and, later, of Bell Atlantic and GTE.

It might appear that the imposition of conditions in such situations is fully in keeping with the way in which the antitrust agencies have come increasingly to handle proposed mergers. Chairman Robert Pitofsky of the Federal Trade Commission recently observed, "[M]erger review [by the antitrust agencies] has become so much a regulatory effort. Relatively few merger cases are fully litigated in the United States courts or the FTC's administrative processes."[82] Instead, the overwhelming majority of them are resolved by negotiated settlements in which the mergers are purged of what the antitrust authorities regard as anticompetitive elements—for example, by agreement of the parties to sell off assets, the combining of which threatens to impair competition.[83]

Despite its substitution of negotiation for litigation, that practice seems consistent with the spirit of the antitrust laws: Section 7 of the Clayton Act concentrates on the possibly anticompetitive effects of changes in an industry's structure consequent on mergers: what the antitrust agencies attempt to do in those quasi-regulatory negotiations is, in principle, identical—to eliminate the aspects of the restructuring effected by the merger that in their judgment threaten competition.

What the FCC did when confronted with the proposed union of SBC and Ameritech might seem essentially similar: it used the lever of its ability to disallow the union to extract from the companies thirty "voluntary" conditions, developed in apparently lengthy and complex negotiations between company representatives and commission staff members. In contrast with the purpose of the settlements secured by the antitrust agencies, however, what the FCC secured in that case were commitments by the parties to *do* certain things, to *behave* in certain ways—subject to possible liability for "voluntary incentive payments to the U.S. Treasury" of as much as $1.125 billion[84]—some of them only remotely and others not even remotely related to the perceived possible injuries to competition *stemming from the merger,* but, in the opinion of three of its five members, likely to be sufficiently *promotive* of competition in *some* respect or, simply, sufficiently socially desirable to make the entire deal in "the public interest."

I allude to that decision with severe qualms, because I have no settled opinion about whether the merger should or should not have been approved or in what ways it might have been restructured to eliminate such threats to competition as it may actually have posed, and have attempted no systematic analysis of the commission's 245-page decision (and 218 pages of appendixes) to see to what extent each of its thirty "volunteered" conditions is rationalized (and, among those, to what extent *persuasively* rationalized) as an offset to or remedy for specific likely anticompetitive effects of the merger. But it is so dramatically illustrative of the temptation of a regulatory commission, in contrast to the antitrust agencies, in a process that is supposed to be deregulatory, to *regulate,* to *prescribe* behavior that it regards as procompetitive (rather than merely to proscribe behavior or structural change that it regards as anticompetitive), to dictate the *results* that it thinks would have been produced by competition *but for* the merger, and to require actions that have nothing to do with competition but that the commission thinks are in "the public interest"—in short, so richly illustrative of the dangers of deregulation going wrong—that I cannot refrain from listing some of the parts of the bargain that seem most egregiously illustrative of that tendency.[85]

In particular, the new SBC–Ameritech entity must set up a separate affiliate to provide all advanced services.[86] Except for Bell Atlantic, which accepted the same handicap as a price for receiving interLATA authority (even though it is not required by the Telecommunications Act,[87] and the company had protested that the handicap would deny it the benefit of substantial economies of scope), the other RBOCs are under no such obligation. In addition, the merging parties agree to "target their deployment of x-DSL services to include low-income groups in rural and urban areas." Specifically, at least 10 percent of their wire centers, both rural and urban, in which they deploy those services "will be low-income wire centers."[88] Moreover, "[t]o offset the loss of probable competition between SBC and Ameritech for residential service in their regions and to facilitate market entry," they commit themselves to offer three promotions of specified amount and duration to all carriers with which they have an interconnection or resale agreement,[89] promotional discounts in their monthly charges for unbundled loops used in providing residential local service,[90] and promotional resale discounts of 32 percent for "not less than 24 months."[91] The applicants also agree to offer "enhanced lifeline plans, [embodying] up to a maximum discount of $10.20 per month."[92] Moreover, "[w]ithin 30 months of the merger closing date the combined firm will enter at least 30 major markets outside SBC's and Ameritech's incumbent service area as a facilities-based carrier of local telecommunications services to business and residential customers. . . . This condition effectively requires SBC and Ameritech to redeem their promise that the merger will form the basis for a new, powerful, truly nationwide multipurpose competitive telecommunications carrier."[93]

Observe that some of those conditions not merely commit the merged entity to refrain from misusing the local monopoly power possessed by *each* of its predecessors in its own market territory to obstruct competition, but require it positively to facilitate competition in ways going beyond the requirements of the Telecommunications Act and, indeed, of the FCC's own rules implementing it: two of them commit the merged entity to offer certain network elements at discounted prices below the commission's own prescribed TELRIC–BS and discounts on sales for resale markedly greater than the commission's own prescription. The rationale set forth in its decision was that both by forestalling potential competition between the merging parties and by extending the geographic scope of the benefits that would accrue to each of them from possible discriminations against competitors, the merger would confer on the combined entity both greater power and greater incentive than each of them would have had separately to preclude competition. Whatever the validity of that prediction, the FCC's order was an intensely *regulatory* response to a merger with such assertedly potential anticompetitive effects.[94]

Moreover, it seems difficult to reconcile the commission's expression of belief that "the merger is likely to have particularly harmful, discriminatory effects on competition in the provision of new types of advanced services"[95] ("high speed, switched, broadband, wire line telecommunications capability that enables users to originate and receive high-quality voice, data, graphics or video telecommunications")[96] and its consequent exaction from the merging parties (both SBC–Ameritech and Bell Atlantic–GTE) of the handicap of providing such advanced services only through separate subsidiaries with its decision, upon the Supreme Court remand of the *Iowa Utilities Board* case, to relieve ILECs from the obligation to share those facilities.[97] It seems impossible to reconcile that requirement also with its approval—at long last—of the applications of SBC and Bell Atlantic for interLATA authority, for Texas and New York, respectively[98]—the prerequisite condition of which was that their local markets be "irreversibly opened to competition."

The commission's exaction from the merging partners also of a "voluntary" promise to offer competitive local exchange service in thirty markets *outside* their respective regions, evidently without even purporting to find a *threat* to competition in those markets stemming from the merger itself, seems particularly egregious, since far from being based on the finding of such a threat, it is rationalized in terms of forcing the companies "to redeem their promise" that the merged entity would be a more effective competitor nationwide. One would have thought that the union of the two companies, far from weakening competition outside their territories, would if anything have enhanced both their ability and their incentive to "go national." Dennis L. Weisman has demonstrated that two merged RBOCs will have a *greater* incentive to enter the territory of a third to provide long-distance service there than would either of them individually, because their union will combine and thereby internalize the benefits of call-back or reverse-traffic elasticity—in the present context, the tendency of calls originating in the invaded RBOC's territory (if provided in the future by the single merged entity) to generate return calls from their previously separate market territories.[99]

Commissioner Powell observed in his powerful partial dissent:

> The approach of rounding up "voluntary" conditions to compensate for largely unrelated potential harms is fraught with public policy problems. . . . I am very uncomfortable with a standard that places harms on one side of the scale and then collects and places any hodge-podge of conditions—no matter how ill-suited to remedying the identified infirmities—on the other side of the scale.
>
> This balancing approach leads to a number of problems: First, the approach creates a great temptation to load up the benefits side of the scale with a big wish list of conditions that are nongermane to the merger's harmful effects. Second, the approach makes it easier for identified harms, even significant ones, to be visited upon the public in exchange for other benefits. Third, the conditions that are sought are more often surrogates for policies and rules of general, rather than merger-specific, applicability, but without the extensive deliberative process and the check of judicial review normally afforded a rulemaking. And fourth, the

process of obtaining "voluntary" conditions inevitably involves bilateral negotiations with the parties that leave the integrity of the Commission's process vulnerable to criticism. . . .

The more serious problem arises with the public interest "scale" . . . when the Commission, rather than weighing the harms against the proffered benefits, attempts to tip the balance by adding weight to the benefits "platter" with conditions—a mountain of goodies designed to leave us, on balance, fat and happy. The public interest standard, as the Commission applies it, does not require that the conditions cure or remedy the identified harms. The conditions need only outweigh the harms.[100]

Anyone with the slightest familiarity with the antitrust laws will need no demonstration that while the difference between the "voluntary" conditions accepted by the FCC in this case and the ones worked out between antitrust authorities and would-be merging parties under Section 7 of the Clayton Act may seem slight, it is fundamental. It was one thing for the Justice Department to have required Bell South and SBC to sell off their wireless businesses in sixteen cities as a condition of its permitting them to set up a joint venture that would have eliminated head-to-head competition between them in those markets—a structural remedy for a structural change—or for the FTC to attach to its approval of the AOL–Time Warner merger the condition that the latter company open its cable systems to nonaffiliated, competing Internet access services—an application of the essential facilities doctrine; it was quite another for the FCC to exact from the two merging RBOCs a promise to produce what could under even the most favorable interpretation be the *results* that, in the Olympian judgment of the regulator, would have been produced but for the possible repression of potential competition caused by the merger; and, so far as many of the conditions are concerned, results that were rather *less* likely or almost certainly would *not* have been forthcoming if the merger were prevented![101]

Asymmetrical Transfer Pricing Rules

I have previously discussed the tendency of regulators to require that when assets are transferred from utility companies to unregulated affiliates operating in markets that either are or are intended to be competitive, the transfer be at book or market value, whichever is higher. Such a rule is compatible neither with consistent regulatory practice nor with a policy of encouraging efficient competition.

The intended asymmetry is probably also futile. While an unregulated affiliate—typically required by regulators to be operated independently of the utility company (to prevent subtle cross-subsidizations)—would presumably be willing to pay market value for those assets when it exceeds book (thereby properly compensating utility ratepayers for the excessive depreciation that they have paid in the past), it is difficult to see how it could be forced to pay book value (thereby excusing utility ratepayers from making good their inadequate past depreciation payments) when it can acquire such assets at a lower price in the market. For the same reason, it is difficult to understand the widespread requirement by regulatory commissions of asymmetrical pricing of goods and services (as distinguished from depreciable assets) transferred between utility company and affiliates—market value or "cost" (evidently typically fully distributed), whichever is *higher,* on transfers from utility to affiliate, and whichever is *lower* from affiliate to utility. How could an unregulated affiliate be expected or ordered to *pay* fully distributed costs, in purchases from the utility or parent, for services it can obtain more cheaply in the market, or to *sell* such goods or services to the utility at cost in circumstances in which it can obtain a higher price in the market? And why *should* it be so ordered in the interest of efficient competition?

Entirely apart from its enforceability, the asymmetrical pricing rule or its frequently encountered alternative, the rule that transfers from utility to affiliate be, simply, at fully distributed cost—rather than incremental cost or Ramsey-efficient levels, both of which are likely to be lower[102]—is of course in the interest neither of consumers (except in the eyes of the "consumer representatives" specializing in utility regulatory practice, who seem to take for granted the superior entitlement of purchasers of utility services over purchasers of unregulated ones)[103] nor of fair or efficient competition in the unregulated markets. What is particularly dismaying is the widely proposed application of that rule even to competition between unregulated electric utility affiliates and their rivals in such unregulated markets as telecommunications[104] or to the provision of heating, air conditioning, or similarly energy-related services, in which the utility companies are the entrants and their rivals (such as the local Bell telephone companies, AT&T, and MCI Worldcom or local cable franchisees, in the former situations, and Sears, General Electric, or Honeywell in the latter) demanding protection against assertedly "unfair" competitive tactics that are the market-dominating incumbents.

Bribing Customers to Leave and Calling It "Competition"

In addition to drafting rules of purportedly fair competitive conduct, the constitution of competitive retail markets for electric power has required resolving the issue of stranded cost recovery (in the process sugar-coating the deal for ratepayers with immediate rate reductions), providing purchasers of utility services who do not choose to leave their historical supplier at least interim protection against the possibility of wide fluctuations in competitive wholesale rates, and specifying the charges customers should escape when they desert their historical retail supplier and shift their patronage to a competitor.

Put another way, the price of the power that continues to be sold by the incumbent distribution company utilities typically comprises three parts: a contribution to the recovery of stranded costs, over some transitional period; a charge for the physical distribution of the power, which it is contemplated will continue to be regulated; and a charge for "standard offer generation service"—or "default service"—to be paid by the customers that remain with their traditional supplier, whether by deliberate choice or out of lethargy. The first of those charges is supposed to be borne by all customers; it is not intended to be escapable by shifting to a competitive retailer or to generation at the consumption site;[105] indeed, if it could be escaped in that way, it would encourage inefficient competition. The second is likewise supposed to be paid uniformly by all customers whose energy continues to be delivered over those local wires. The third component is therefore at one and the same time the charge for the "default service"—that is, for the power itself, paid only by the customers that remain—and, by the same token, the portion of the retail price that is to be returned, in the form of a "shopping credit," to customers who choose no longer to take that service. In other words, the "shopping credit" *is* the price of the "standard offer service"—paid by those who continue to take that service and avoided by those who cease to do so.[106]

The setting of the shopping credit provides an obvious temptation to regulators to encourage competitors artificially. The California Public Utility Commission steadfastly declined to succumb. The Pennsylvania commission, to cite the outstanding example to date at the other extreme, deliberately prescribed a credit large enough to produce something like a 10 percent rate reduction for customers who shifted to competitive marketers; and one of its commissioners then boasted that as a result more customers had shifted in that state than in the entire remainder of the country. He then advised the New Jersey commission, with only partial success, to outdo Pennsylvania, simply by increasing the size of the bribe, evidently in the belief that he had discovered the secret of perpetual motion.

What would be the credit necessary to ensure that the resulting competition was efficient? Manifestly—at least to an economist—it would be equated to the cost that the utility company actually avoids when it loses a customer: essentially the spot price of purchases from the pool plus some, presumably very small, retailing costs (including losses, taxes, and the like but no costs of marketing or customer acquisition, because the standard or default service would not be marketed).[107] That would be the margin within which the competing retail marketer would have to operate if it were to compete successfully, so long as it offered the same services as the utility company. Clearly, any competitors with incremental costs higher than those of the incumbent would be unable to offer buyers a price sufficiently low to induce them to shift. Nor should they be, since their taking over the function of serving customers would impose costs on society greater than the costs it would save by consumers' shifting to them.

It may well be—indeed, consumer inertia makes it highly likely—that an inducement to customers to shift equal only to the costs that their historical suppliers would save would not create much of an opportunity for competitors. If so, that would be the case because the mere resale of electric power, purchasable by incumbents and challengers alike from regional power pools at (it is hoped) a competitive wholesale price, offers comparatively few opportunities for creative or socially useful competition, so long as the retail prices of the incumbent are frozen.[108] The real opportunities for aggressive and innovative competitors selling electric power are likely to emerge, if at all, only when the utility price caps come off—at which point consumers will be looking for protection from the risks of what could be highly volatile wholesale markets[109]—and in bundling sales of power with other energy-related services—audits, conservation, climate control, load management, and the supply and servicing of energy-using equipment.

To the extent that a competitor can offer additional services of that kind, which customers value sufficiently to pay the additional cost of providing them, it can of course charge them more than the credit they receive from the utility company upon their departure and compete effectively. In either case, consumers would be making the unbiased choices, depending upon whether those additional services were or were not worth the additional cost of offering them.

Since a credit in excess of actually avoided costs is a subsidy, it is the economist's responsibility to point out who will be paying for it. There are only two possibilities.

One candidate is the incumbent utility distribution company. "Bigger shopping credits create greater consumer savings," said the aforementioned Pennsylvania regulator, clearly implying that the burden would fall on that company. The more it pays the customers it loses than the costs it saves by their leaving, the less it will have left over. That reasoning is, however, either naïve or disingenuous. If a commission, having frozen rates at a level it considers sufficient to permit recovery of some predetermined proportion of the costs likely to be stranded, then introduces a shopping credit with a built-in subsidy, the commission is clearly altering the terms of the stranded cost bargain. In any event, if a state decides to permit a utility company recovery of something less than 100 percent of its stranded costs, the obvious and only fair way to do so is to order it to reduce rates to all its customers, not just to the ones who desert it.[110]

Recall that the shopping credit *is* the price of the standard offer or default service: it is what default customers pay for remaining with their traditional supplier and what shifters avoid. The larger the credit, the more it costs customers to remain with the local utility company. If in those circumstances the local utility is kept whole—that is, is permitted to recover its agreed-upon total stranded costs—the only other possible source of the subsidy is the customers who remain with it. Since they are typically going to be the smaller, less well-informed, lower-income customers, what kind of equitable purpose would that serve?[111]

****

Since I doubtless owe my appearance on this happy occasion in major part to my Walter Mitty experience at the New York Public Service Commission and at the Civil Aeronautics Board, I fear that there is an element of ungraciousness in my message about the mistakes regulators and other policymakers are prone to make in managing the transition from regulation to deregulation. If I seem to have demonstrated that the passage from one role to the other involves merely a transition from presumption to smugness, I can only offer my assurance that I would be terrified if I had to manage that transition. As I have suggested elsewhere (but only once!), if called to account for my performance, I would be tempted to give the kind of answer Yogi Berra gave when asked why he had missed three consecutive fly balls while substituting in the outfield: "Hank Bauer's screwed up right field so bad, nobody can play the position!"

Notes

This is a revised and expanded version of the lecture delivered in December 1999. Since this monograph draws heavily on—indeed, in a sense encapsulates—work that I have done over at least the past twenty years, much of it in collaboration with Timothy J. Tardiff, there is a sense in which he is effectively a coauthor of large sections of it—additionally because of his extremely helpful suggestions and criticisms of the present version. At the same time, the analysis is clearly mine, and I must bear full responsibility for it. I express my gratitude also to Robert E. Litan and Dennis L. Weisman for their thoroughgoing criticisms and suggestions and to Jaime D'Almeida for his invaluable research assistance.

1. It was no accident, therefore, that I was, to my chagrin, scooped in the first self-conscious attempt to adopt such principles by the Wisconsin Public Service Commission, under the farsighted chairmanship of Richard (now Judge) Cudahy, in its *Madison Gas* decision in the spring of 1974, in which the principal protagonist-witnesses were Charles Cicchetti and Edward Berlin, testifying on behalf of the Environmental Defense Fund, and my esteemed former student, Irwin Stelzer (*Madison Gas & Electric* 1974). See also Kahn (1974 and 1975).

2. See Kahn (1982) and Kearney and Merrill (1998).

3. One of the happy aspects of my earlier experiences in the regulatory arena, which occurred while I was, successively, a professor, college dean, and then chairman of two independent regulatory commissions, is that they occurred for the most part before I was exposed to the perils of consultancy—which have ever since forced me continually to pose to myself the question, "Does where I stand depend upon where I sit?" In point of fact, I had during the period of preparing my two volumes (Kahn 1970 and 1971) been exposed to those perils, having served for some five years as a

member, along with William J. Baumol and Otto Eckstein, of AT&T's first Council of Economic Advisers. In that role, I tried to maintain my independence, however, by devoting my major attention to developing what I referred to as "a grand competitive strategy for the Bell System"—counseling the company to welcome competition while at the same time demanding equivalent, accommodating reforms of the regulation to which it was subject—the first part of which advice the company essentially ignored; the result, as they say, is history.

In contrast, much of what I have to say here comes from my frequent participation during the past two decades in adversarial proceedings, mainly on behalf of the regional Bell operating companies, electric distribution companies, and rail shippers. To this necessary disclosure, the implications of which, as I say, I find myself frequently examining, I attach the—inevitably self-serving—mitigating considerations that, first, the market for consultants places a high value on consistency, enforced by the process of cross-examination; and, second, a client therefore tends to seek out consultants whose previous public declarations, preferably unpaid, seem consistent with the positions it hopes to persuade them to take. In consequence, where a consultant stands tends—indeed, it had damned well better tend—to depend upon where he or she had *previously* sat.

Still, I am compelled to agree with Roger G. Noll's expression of regret that "partisan advocacy . . . has become the dominant method that economists use to communicate with regulatory policymakers." See Noll (1999, 4 and 26).

4. See Kahn (1998) and Kahn (1984b), respectively.

5. See Federal Communications Commission (1996a and 1996b). I have already bitterly criticized that perverse application of marginal cost pricing principles in several forums (Kahn 1998; and Kahn, Tardiff, and Weisman 1999), but it so perfectly exemplifies the phenomenon I have memorialized in the title I have given this monograph that I am compelled to summarize those among the criticisms that illustrate it.

6. I have elsewhere (see note 5, above) explained the fallacy of the commission's explicit assumption (Federal Communications Commission 1996b, par. 693) that its TELRIC–BS, with the long run defined as the theoretical extreme in which all costs are variable, is the level at which a perfectly competitive market would set prices, citing William J. Fellner's observation, many decades ago, that firms in such markets would systematically practice "antici-

patory retardation" in investing in the newest, lowest-cost technology. See also Kahn (1970, vol. 1, 119). I have also, in those expositions, cited Jerry A. Hausman's advice to the FCC that the competitive price would in those circumstances have to incorporate a gross rate of return (including provision for economic depreciation) far higher than traditional public utility levels—advice that the commission and the several state commissions have evidently systematically ignored. See the summary of the several Hausman studies explicating and estimating those required returns in Crandall and Hausman (2000, 87–89). See also Tardiff (1999).

7. For example, the FCC has decided, in the context of determining the requisite universal service subsidy for nonrural ILECs, that the TELRIC calculation requires the assumption that an ILEC serve current demand always with new switches, the cost of which, on a per-line basis, is lower than the "growth modules"—switch hardware added to existing switches—that they typically use to expand their capacity. Vendors of switches typically charge lower prices on new switches, on a per-line basis, than on growth modules because they want to encourage ILECs to lock themselves into the use of their modules for future expansion. See Federal Communications Commission (1999c, pars. 317 and 319). The result is to understate grossly the cost that even the constructor and operator of the hypothetically most efficiently designed system will actually incur, even when the higher future costs (of the growth modules) are reduced to present-value terms.

   At least one state (Delaware) has decided to follow that same rule for the mandated pricing of switches (sustained in *Bell Atlantic Delaware v. Robert J. McMahon, Chairman, et al.,* 80 F. Supp. 2d 218, 2000), and other states are now being urged to do the same. On the other hand, according to the FCC, "at least one state public service commission . . . has taken the [higher] cost of growth modules into account," citing *AT&T v. FCC,* 220 F.3d 607, 616–18 (D.C. Cir. 2000), No. 99-1538 (filed September 15, 2000). See Federal Communications Commission (2000d, 48).

8. So after contending strenuously, a year and a half before the FCC adopted its TELRIC–BS standard, that network elements should be priced at the actual incremental cost to the incumbent firms, on the ground, among others, that

   > only a new firm can write on a blank slate; and once it has done so, it too will never again be in a position to do so again on the basis of the latest technology. Nor would it be economic for it to do so:

> what it must seek to do is minimize the additional current and
> future costs (in present value terms) *given* the plant and equipment
> already in its possession (Kahn 1995, 18–19),

I asserted explicitly that this would be true even if the incumbent
firm was inefficient. The proper penalty for such inefficiency, I
said, would be a reduction in the regulatorily prescribed markup
above incremental cost required to permit recovery of total costs
so long as it was still regulated (Kahn 1995, 6–7), just as it would
be penalized by competition once it was deregulated. (I will apol-
ogize only this one time for regarding this forum as not an inappropriate occasion for drawing heavily on my own work in the
past.)

9. At the same time, I cannot flatly reject Robert W. Crandall's conclusion, on the basis of the sad experience on which I comment
here, that the only escape from endless regulation is going to be to
get the regulators entirely out of that business, which he characterizes as "a substitution of regulation for investment [by competi-
tors] in production facilities" (Crandall 2000, 48). See also Litan
and Noll (1998) and Kahn (1998, chap. 7, "The Marasmus of the
FCC").

10. For a suggestion of the radical difference between the results that
would be produced under typical rate caps, with productivity
adjustments, and the results produced by the FCC's prescriptions,
see Kahn, Tardiff, and Weisman (1999, 331–32).

In the midst of the general enthusiasm for rate-cap regulation
during at least the past decade, to which I have contributed, it is
important to remind ourselves that while it comes closer than
cost-based regulation to mimicking the competitive process in the
incentives it offers utility company monopolists to improve their
efficiency, that enhanced incentive to cut costs at the same time
jeopardizes the quality of their service. See, for example, "Local
Phone Companies Put Customer Service on Hold, Critics Charge,"
Wall Street Journal, July 6, 2000.

In effect, the shift to rate caps assumes that regulators can mon-
itor and control service quality more effectively than efficiency;
but it is clearly a poor substitute for competition in that respect—
and, indeed, for traditional cost-plus regulation itself. See, for
example, Kahn (1970, vol. 1, 23–25, and 1971, vol. 2, 50, 53,
97).

11. See Justice Stephen Breyer's concurrence and dissent in *AT&T
Corp. v. Iowa Utilities Board*, 525 U.S. 366 (1999), 425–26, Ben W.

Lewis in Lyon and Abramson (1940, 691), and Santayana's predicted fate of "[t]hose who cannot remember the past."

12. *AT&T Corp. v. Iowa Utilities Board,* 525 U.S. 366 (1999), 429, emphasis added.

13. See, for example, Kahn (1999c, 7–10).

14. See Tardiff (1999, 187).

15. See the illuminating characterization of this anomaly by Hausman and Sidak (1999, 463–64) as the FCC's requiring the ILECs to confer on CLECs a "valuable option" of leasing assets for periods of time shorter than their economic life without compensation for the risk of obsolescence.

16. See Crandall (1999).

17. In my declaration to the FCC in its proceedings on the remand from the Supreme Court, in which the issue was the criteria to be applied in determining which network elements were to be shared—and from which, for the reasons I have just mentioned, price was not at issue—I insisted that in economic reality the two cannot be separated. With apologies for quoting myself (in turn, in effect quoting my former teacher, Schumpeter), I insisted:

> In considering the Commission's sharing rules, therefore, the economic reality is
>
> • that while the obligation to share whatever network elements competitors demand in itself violates the principle that in a deregulated world innovation requires the prospect of exclusive enjoyment of the fruits of successful ventures, the *price* at which sharing is mandated, if it is to be mandated at all, becomes an essential part of the equation;
>
> • in these circumstances, the Commission's prescription of a price purportedly equal to the minimum costs that would be incurred by an efficient supplier, using the most modern technology and writing, as it were, on a clean slate, completes the process of destroying the incentive to innovate. The notion that the ILECs are likely to find it profitable to engage in such unprecedentedly risky investments as they now contemplate—the most notable example being the digitalization of subscriber lines—under a regulatory regime that requires them immediately to share those facilities with any and all competitors who ask for them—competitors who are subject to no such obligation—at prices based on the Commission's hypothetical, most-efficient-firm cost standard seems flatly in conflict with the long-run prerequisites of innovation.

For the support of that assertion, I cited a study, reported in the *Economist* of February 20, 1999, which found an overall rate of return for some seventeen successful innovations in the 1970s averaging 56 percent and comparing that with the 16 percent average return on investment for all American business over the previous thirty years. Even more directly pertinent, I suggested, would be a comparison with the traditional regulatorily prescribed rates of depreciation and return typically incorporated in the models on the basis of which the FCC and state commissions had been purporting to measure the TELRICs that the FCC prescribed for the pricing of UNEs (Kahn 1999c, 5, n. 1).

The commission was evidently persuaded by considerations such as these, so far as ILEC investments in digitalization are concerned, as I proceed to point out.

18. *Iowa Utilities Board et al. v. Federal Communications Commission,* 219 F. 3d 744 (2000).
19. *AT&T Corp. v. Iowa Utilities Board,* 525 U.S. 366 (1999), 428–29.
20. See Federal Communications Commission (1999d).
21. They were particularly outraged by the approval by several commissions of AT&T's demand for a "platform"—that is, that the ILECs provide them an assembly of UNEs sufficient to permit them to offer complete retail services, at TELRIC–BS prices. As the ILECs protested, that offered the CLECs a means of reselling the services of the incumbents alternative to the one provided for in the Telecommunications Act, under a different pricing arrangement. By so doing, it gave them an opportunity to game the system—choosing the platform route, at TELRIC–BS, to sell services whose prices regulators had been holding far *above* cost to cross-subsidize basic residential rates; and choosing the resale route, at wholesale discounts prescribed by the FCC—as I point out in the following section—at the total avoided costs of retailing rather than the much smaller costs actually avoided by the incumbents, for services whose prices regulators were holding *below* any pertinent measure of costs. See also n. 107 below.
22. See Federal Energy Regulatory Commission (1996, 49–50):

> The Commission's goal is to ensure that customers have the benefits of competitively priced generation. However, we must do so without abandoning our traditional obligation to ensure that utilities have a fair opportunity to recover prudently incurred costs and that they maintain power supply reliability. As well, the benefits of competition should not come at the expense of other customers. The Commission believes that requiring utilities to provide non-discriminatory open access transmission tariffs, while simultaneously resolving the extremely difficult issue of recovery of transition costs

(discussed infra), is the key to reconciling these competing demands.

23. See Weisman (1997). See also Kahn, Tardiff, and Weisman (1999, 337–42).

24. See Baumol, Ordover, and Willig (1996, par. 25).

25. See, for example, Kahn (1970, vol. 1, 155, 164). Although my own endorsement of that proposition has been slightly less unequivocal (see ibid., 175–80, and 1971, vol. 2, 246–50) and it is possible to make a case for restrictions on that pricing freedom on "infant company" grounds—for a strong exposition see Bhagwat (1999)—I am unaware of any serious contention that the relevant standard is anything other than the actual incremental costs of the incumbent.

26. To the extent that the ILECs were to be entitled also to recover sunk costs reflecting inadequate depreciation of the investment costs of acquiring those UNEs, similarly, efficient competition would require that they be collected equiproportionately from all providers.

27. When the issue of setting the rates for cable companies attaching their lines to the poles of the telephone companies came before the New York commission during my chairmanship and the question arose of the possible desirability of setting them at incremental costs, I recall distinctly—to my present chagrin—insisting that they be set, instead, at fully distributed costs. In hindsight, I presume that I was succumbing to the tendency of a regulator to be concerned principally about the welfare of purchasers of the services for whose prices he or she would be held responsible and accepting the rationalization that there was no particular reason to confer the benefits of economies of scale or scope disproportionately on the purchasers of services outside my jurisdiction. It was only later that I came more clearly to recognize that considerations of efficiency would have dictated the application of Ramsey principles: since the demand for the services of the newly emerging "community antenna television" providers was undoubtedly more elastic than for basic telephone dial-tone services, I should have recognized the validity of proposals that the rates for the former services be set closer to incremental costs, as I have come explicitly to recognize and advocate in other contexts since then. See Kahn (1998, 82–89, and especially 86, n. 118). See also Kahn (1996b).

Had the cable operators and phone companies been direct competitors in the offer of telephone service, however, I believe that my prescription of charging the former the same fully distributed costs as were the basis on which the incumbents' telephone rates were set would have been the correct prescription. See Kahn (1970, vol. 1, 174–75).

28. See Kahn (1998, 96–99).

29. See Federal Communications Commission (1999d).

30. These are the "necessary" and "impair" standards prescribed by the Telecommunications Act for identifying the network elements to be subject to mandatory sharing. It is not clear to me whether this logic of separately identifying and costing those two inputs is confounded by the transition from circuit-switched to packet-switched technology and substitution of Voice over Internet Protocol (VoIP) for what is now basic service. What this prospect does suggest, however, is the foolishness of continuing regulatory prescription and represcription in the context of so rapidly changing a technology.

31. See the exposition in Kahn (1998, 73–76) of the identical logic as applied—fallaciously—to the familiar and long-standing controversies over whether subscriber dial tone is a "separate service," with its cost to be recovered in a separate charge, or an essential input to the provision, for example, of long-distance and local usage, with its costs properly recovered in the charges for those services.

32. See Kahn (1999c, pars. 17–18).

33. See Kahn (1984a) and Kahn and Shew (1987). The statement in the text describes the historical situation; I refrain from speculating about whether spectrum sharing alters the efficient pricing solution from one to *two* lump-sum charges.

34. See Federal Communications Commission (1999d, pars. 138–140).

35. See ibid., pars. 139–141.

36. See ibid., pars. 151–152.

37. For a powerful—and, as my ensuing exposition makes clear, in my view extreme—statement of that position, see Hausman and Sidak (1999).

38. See Areeda (1989, 852).

39. *United States v. Aluminum Co. of America*, 148 F. 2d. 416 (1945), 430. That decision also contains the admonition against a monopoly's being condemned if the monopoly power was "thrust upon" its possessor, or if it had survived merely by virtue of its "superior skill, foresight, and industry." Ibid., 429–30.

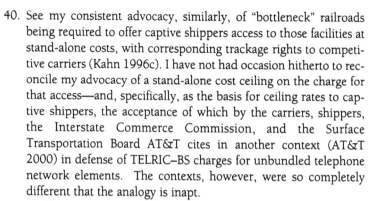

40. See my consistent advocacy, similarly, of "bottleneck" railroads being required to offer captive shippers access to those facilities at stand-alone costs, with corresponding trackage rights to competitive carriers (Kahn 1996c). I have not had occasion hitherto to reconcile my advocacy of a stand-alone cost ceiling on the charge for that access—and, specifically, as the basis for ceiling rates to captive shippers, the acceptance of which by the carriers, shippers, the Interstate Commerce Commission, and the Surface Transportation Board AT&T cites in another context (AT&T 2000) in defense of TELRIC–BS charges for unbundled telephone network elements. The contexts, however, were so completely different that the analogy is inapt.

The Staggers Act, deregulating the railroads, was predicated upon the universal recognition of their need for greater freedom to discriminate in their charges for different kinds of traffic, if they were to have an opportunity to recover both their heavy sunk costs and their large element of fixed and common costs, even on a forward-looking basis.

At the same time, there was concern about the danger of the railroads' exploiting the very large amounts of captive traffic, where they concededly had and still enjoy a large amount of monopoly power. The central question, therefore, concerned the proper *upper limit* for permissible price discrimination.

The Staggers Act had itself adopted a standard approximately the same as the one proposed by the ILECs for the pricing of UNEs—namely, the actual (rather than hypothetical) long-run incremental costs of the carriers. The railroads had developed a system of accounting that attempted in an approximate sort of way to measure those costs—their so-called Form A costs—which included both variable and a proxy for incremental capital costs. The act set a ceiling for individual rates rising within a few years to 180 percent of those costs—below which rates would be presumed to be acceptable—that is, to involve an acceptable and/or necessary level of discrimination.

For testing contested rates *above* that level, the major parties accepted the theoretical validity of the conception, expounded among others by Professors William J. Baumol and Robert D. Willig, that blank-slate stand-alone costs—the prospective costs of constructing a most efficient, entirely new system to serve the needs of any grouping of customers—were the proper, theoretically correct limit of acceptable price discrimination, because rates in excess of that level would, in a perfectly contestable market (that is, with totally free entry) not survive. There was absolutely no conception that such ceilings or stand-alone costs would be *below* the actual LRIC or TSLRIC of the railroads: on the contrary, the expectation was that they would be markedly higher, would be applicable only to rates exceeding 180 percent of those *actual LRICs* but would set a limit to the extent to which they could be *higher*. Nor, therefore, was there any proffered justification, explicit or implicit, that they could be used to disallow inefficiencies reflected in the Form A costs themselves.

Moreover, there was no conception of the railroad industry's being subject to so rapidly improving a technology that a grounds-up TSLRIC for any group of customers would be *lower* than the actual long-run incremental costs of the railroads for that traffic, whether TS or merely LRIC, even though they might be below some measure of average book or historic costs, and no consideration of what kind of return would be proper in those circumstances.

Finally, the captive shipper ceilings, so defined, while invoked in several cases, have proved hopelessly difficult to administer, with the result that the captive shippers clause itself has provided little protection and is only rarely invoked these days.

41. Some of the distribution companies on whose behalf I have testified in "code of conduct" proceedings have, however, accepted the obligation, if they use their utility bills to bill also for their competitive affiliates—presumably at very low incremental costs—to offer that same service, at the same rates, to competitors of those affiliates; if they use their billing envelopes to include promotional material on behalf of the former, that they offer to do the same for the latter; and in bidding on major customer projects involving a combination of new or additional regulated distribution facilities along with sales of electric power and competitive equipment or services, that they be prepared to submit such proposals jointly with unaffiliated as well as with affiliated energy service companies.

42. See Coase (1937) and Williamson (1979).

43. So, for example, the FCC in its decision approving the merger of SBC and Ameritech, with numerous conditions obliging the merged company to facilitate local competition, empowered the chief of its Common Carrier Bureau to authorize an independent arbitrator to resolve disputes over the adequacy of its compliance (Federal Communications Commission 1999b, par. 383).

44. For example, one exponent of those models attributed to tele-phone service only one quarter of the cost of poles and other con-duits, on the ground that in a system newly constructed from scratch, a much larger portion would be used for electric and cable service than is actually used today (Hatfield Model Release 3.1, Model Description, Hatfield Associates, Inc., February 28, 1997, appendix B, 52). The blank-slate assumption evidently requires, logically, that those other, nontelephone companies be assumed to be writing on such a slate as well. See the fuller discussion of this example in Kahn (1998, 94–96, n. 137).

45. For a description of the "striking difference between the fractious, discordant, litigation-dominated American implementation process and the low-keyed, industry-regulator-mediated approach adopted in Canada" and an observation that the "innovative and flexible [Canadian] process has worked very well up to this point," citing "truly impressive advances on the road towards local com-petition by employing innovative nonadversary mediation tech-niques," see Janisch (1998).

46. See Grimm and Winston (2000).

47. See Hausman and Sidak (1999, 463–66).

48. See Hahn (1999, 1). See also Thierer (1999).

49. Crandall and Hausman (2000, 18) introduced a Schumpeterian consideration, the importance of which I cannot appraise, that could counsel against enforced sharing even of the ILECs' copper loops:

> If an incumbent local network operator leases part of its current network to its rivals, will it be able to adopt new technology with-out these rivals' (entrants') assent? Surely, one would not want these new competitors using the regulatory process simply to delay or frustrate their rivals' attempts to innovate. . . . Once a new local telecommunications entrant begins to offer service using its rival's local loops, switches, and network intelligence, it has every incen-tive to demand that these facilities not be altered (86–87).

50. One aspect of these benefits that we have emphasized stems from the economies of scope of combining local and interLATA serv-ices—such as, similarly, motivate long-distance companies to offer a full range of local services, wired and wireless. InterLATA entry of the RBOCs promises especial benefit to the small users of toll service, who have unquestionably benefited far less than large cus-tomers from the increasing competitiveness of the long-distance business, because the local exchange companies already serve all of them and therefore need not duplicate the fixed costs of serving

them, even if they place no toll calls. Apparently unintentionally, Frederick R. Warren-Boulton (1998, 12), testifying before the Kansas Corporation Commission on behalf of AT&T and MCI in opposition to the petition by SWB for relief from the interLATA restriction, corroborated that prediction by pointing out that the Southern New England Telephone Company, SNET, had already, as of 1998, taken over 34 percent of the interLATA customers in its territory and 12 percent of the revenues: just as the interexchange carriers have for good economic reasons concentrated their competition on the big, especially big business, customers, so the ILECs are likely to have the greatest success with customers with small toll billings.

51. In view of the necessity of ILECs' cooperating actively in opening their local markets, the assertion of Hausman and Sidak (1999, 430) that retention of "the regulatory quarantine as a bargaining chip for regulators" is "superfluous" because "the 1996 legislation expressly mandated unbundled access to the local network for competitors" seems ingenuous. See the strong argument to that effect by Schwartz (2000): that regulation alone is far less likely to be effective in setting up the complex, novel arrangements required to provide equal opportunities to competitors at the local level than it had been in securing equal access arrangements for long-distance carriers; and that it was therefore necessary to withhold the interLATA carrot to ensure the wholehearted cooperation of the incumbents.

52. See Federal Communications Commission (1999e).

53. See Schwartz (1997, par. 70), emphasis added.

54. See ibid., pars. 20 and 80.

55. See ibid., par. 21.

56. See Bernheim and Willig (1994). This asserted threat to competition arises, however, only if the ILEC at the terminating end can distinguish calls coming to it over the interexchange carrier's trunk by the identity of the ILEC at the originating end; the RBOCs maintain that they cannot do so.

57. At the end of 1999, cable modems served 71 percent of the 1.7 million customers using high-speed access, and DSL served 29 percent (Federal Communications Commission 2000a).

58. See Kahn (1998, chap. 1, "Where the Money Is: The Temptation of the Kleptocrats"). See also Kahn (1996a and 1997).

59. See Kahn (1985).

60. See Joskow (2000a). A relevant consideration in deciding what would constitute a fair resolution, it seems to me, is the fact that

the market value of electric utility companies' stocks has on average over the past forty-five years markedly exceeded book value—suggesting earnings in excess of the cost of capital. Such a rationalization of something less than 100 percent recovery takes on the aspect of "retroactive ratemaking"—retroactive correction of previous rate decisions that turned out excessively generous or meager—which has generally not been regarded as good regulatory practice. The economic reason for that taboo, however—that, by making the regulatory process more perfectly cost-plus in character, such a practice would severely dilute the companies' incentives to be maximally efficient—clearly does not apply where, as has typically been the case, the settling out of sunk-cost-recovery issues is accompanied by freezes, indexations, or total deregulation of rates thenceforward.

61. See Baumol, Joskow, and Kahn (1995, 46–47, 49–54); and Baumol and Sidak (1995).

62. See Joskow (2000b, 132). The utilities had emphasized from the outset the importance of their willing rather than reluctant cooperation in the restructuring process and its dependence on such a promise. On the necessity of filling the gaps and closing the loopholes in the attempts to recover the costs in this way, see Gordon and Olson (1999).

63. Lehman and Weisman (2000) have found a strong, statistically significant tendency of state commissions that have adopted price-cap regulation to renege on the commitments implicit in such incentive regulation by prescribing terms more inviting of competitive entry—in particular, lower charges for subscriber loops made available to competitors—than commissions practicing rate-base, rate-of-return regulation or qualifying the price caps with sharing of surplus (or deficient) profits with ratepayers. That finding confirmed a suggestion by Weisman considerably earlier (1994) that profit sharing would, by giving commissions a vested interest in the profitability of incumbent firms, cause them to be more conservative about opening their markets to competitive entry than pure price-cap states. Lehman and Weisman characterize such regulatory behavior as opportunistic. It seems to me likely, on the other hand, that the active advocacy by the ILECs of moving to price-cap regulation probably reflected a comparable opportunism on their part, because they had knowledge superior to that of regulators about the opportunities for reducing their costs and increasing their profits under such a regime.

64. See Joskow (2000a).

65. Although I have not had the opportunity to attempt to assess the extent to which those contrasting expectations have been fulfilled in the several states that have or have not deregulated their electric utility industries, it would be embarrassing if I were not to allude, at least, to the catastrophic consequences in California, which clearly thought it belonged to the first group of states, shortly after deregulation. Clearly, the preconditions for successful deregulation peculiar to that industry were not met in that case; it does not seem to me an overreaction to question, on the basis of that unhappy experience, whether they ever can be.

In any event, the subsequent explosion of wholesale prices, under the influence of soaring prices of natural gas and NO_x emissions permits and the simple failure of capacity to keep up with rapidly expanding demand, may be regarded as the just reward of ratepayers and legislators for the opportunism they displayed in pressing for deregulation. Just as traditional regulation had held rates markedly below competitive levels during the inflations of the 1970s and far above in the 1980s and 1990s—generating the strong political pressures for deregulation—so continued regulation would probably once again have held them below such levels in the altered circumstances of the past few years—and probably the next few as well.

66. See, for example, Kahn (1984b).

67. Defining type I errors as disallowing actions that are actually socially beneficial and type II as permitting actions by utility companies that do indeed unfairly and inefficiently burden purchasers of regulated services, competitors in unregulated markets, or both, Costello characterizes that proclivity of regulators as "a tendency to make their overwhelming priority the avoidance" of the latter (Costello 2000, 58).

68. See Kahn (1998, 35–47, 82–89).

69. See Lipsky and Sidak (1999, 1222–23), who contended that courts are ill-equipped to perform this function.

70. The airlines have been explicitly exempted from the corresponding authority of the Federal Trade Commission to act against unfair methods of competition in industry generally.

71. See Kahn (1999a).

72. See Transportation Research Board/National Research Council (1999, especially 6–10, 81–96).

73. What follows is in part a summary of Kahn (1999a).

74. See Kahn (1979, 11–12).

75. See Morrison and Winston (1987, 53); and Hurdle et al. (1989).

76. As Professors Baumol and Willig have pointed out time and again, the stand-alone cost ceiling would automatically be enforced under the Utopian perfect contestability that they posit: it would pay entrants to come in and serve any group of consumers being charged more than that (Baumol, Panzar, and Willig 1982, 508–9). See also note 40, above.

77. Morrison and Winston (2000), whose previous magisterial work on the consequences of airline deregulation makes whatever they have to say on the subject impossible to dismiss, have purported to demonstrate that, judged by the consequent injury to consumers (as they have measured it), predation has been of little—indeed, negligible—importance: "Even when an alleged instance of predatory behavior has ended, average fares on a route do not rise" (Morrison and Winston 2000, 30). And "alleged predatory behavior [has] not elevated fares" (32).

The authors have, in private communications, confirmed that the foregoing summaries are of their estimates in which their criterion and measure of successful predation was whether and to what extent fares ended up *higher* than their levels *before entry* of the putative victims. I submit that such a criterion is at best partial: the typical claim of predation—and that of the Department of Transportation, whose report set off most of this controversy (April 1998, 160)—is satisfied if the questionable tactics succeed in permitting mere *restoration* of fares to their preentry levels. That mere restoration would impose a zero cost on consumers, according to their calculation.

Morrison and Winston (2000) have further responded that they have also recognized in their tests that "carriers could still benefit from an alleged predatory strategy if preentry fares on those routes were higher than fares on otherwise comparable routes," but they found "that the benefits [thus measured] are small." As they summarized the results of their inquiry: "Even if one accepts the Transportation Department's definition of predatory behavior, predation has not hurt travelers. . . . [A]lthough fares return to their original level after predation ends, the gain to carriers from elevated fares on these routes amounts to only $20 million annually" (35).

In that calculation, "elevated" means not "raised" from their putatively predatory levels, but raised to levels "higher than fares on otherwise comparable routes," with the measure of the costs of predation only the extent to which the preentry fares were unusually high.

That second measure still has the effect of ignoring the phenomenon insofar as the putatively predatory response to competitive entry permits restoration of fares on the challenged routes to preentry levels that were *not* "higher than . . . on otherwise comparable routes," even though it eliminates the threatened competitive undermining of the industry's generally prevailing fare levels and highly discriminatory fare structure. Moreover, the Morrison and Winston database of those "otherwise comparable routes" excludes routes served by Southwest Airlines, apparently because they used it originally to determine the presence or absence of a "hub premium," and the authors felt the inclusion of Southwest's routes, which do not typically involve hubs dominated by incumbent carriers, distorted that comparison. Since, however, according to their calculations elsewhere, Southwest's competition has accounted for more than 52 percent of all the "savings from lower real fares since deregulation" attributable to competition—as distinguished from decreases that they attribute to "improvements in carriers' operating efficiencies" (Winston 1998, 101)—its exclusion from the base with which restored fares on routes putatively subject to predation are compared clearly drastically reduces the calculated costs of that predation to consumers, even according to their own extremely restricted criterion.

Finally, as is widely recognized, an additional possible benefit of successful predation—albeit not measurable—is, by setting an example of the response that awaits would-be challengers, to increase the hesitation of others in the future; and there is no reason in principle why that demonstration effect would be expected to eventuate in increases in fares of the putative predators on the particular contested route only, rather than generally. So that effect, too, simply does not enter into their calculations of the cost to consumers of putatively predatory tactics.

78. I wrote (Kahn 1999a, 7):

> The spokesmen for the major carriers profess to be shocked by the DOT's suggestion that they be prohibited in these circumstances from expanding their flight frequencies, which would deny them the right to satisfy the expansion of demand for their services set off by the newly introduced price competition. In effect, they protest, the DOT would force them to ration their services. . . . The simple and, in my opinion, sufficient answers are that the "yield management" . . . *had already*—and, so far as I know, close to universally—*entailed just such rationing.* . . . The "rationing" that the major carriers now accuse the DOT of forcing them to practice is

no different in kind from the policies they already follow ubiquitously. Presumably, like the Claude Rains character in *Casablanca,* they would be "shocked, shocked" to find that rationing was going on in their establishments, just before having their winnings handed to them by their yield-manager croupiers.

Those spokesmen have at times asserted that explicit rationing, eventuating in an inability or failure of carriers to satisfy demand for discounted seats on particular flights, is comparatively unimportant; that the principal tool of yield management is the establishment of conditions—such as a Saturday night stayover, advance purchase, or penalties for changes—that limit the demand itself. The simple response is that the establishment of such conditions still constitutes rationing: the conditions are the particular method that carriers use to accomplish it.

The criticism of the DOT's proposed restrictions on incumbent carriers' responding to competitive entry by increasing their capacity or the number of discounted seats they offer—in one instance cited by DOT, they were increased from fewer than 1,500 during the quarter immediately before competitive entry to almost 50,000 during the next three-month period, and in the very next quarter, after departure of the challenger, cut to fewer than 1,000—is of course not confined to the complaint that they in effect impose rationing: the core criticism is that they would interfere with an important part of the competitive process itself. The difference in views between—to put it roughly—critics and defenders of the DOT initiative comes down to a difference in their assessments of the importance, as part of a competitive process, of highly pinpointed *responses* of incumbents to increases in demand set off by competitive entry limited in duration to the survival of a challenger and of protecting the initiating price-cutting entry that stimulates the demand in the first place. Of course, there is the additional difficulty of predicting, in enforcement actions, which of those vigorous competitive responses will prove to be temporary and which not.

79. Despite the more or less even division of the members of the Transportation Research Board's Committee for the Study of Competition in the U.S. Airline Industry on whether the DOT should be encouraged to proceed with its independent enforcement actions or defer to the Department of Justice, all members recognized the critical relevance of opportunity costs in those circumstances (Transportation Research Board/National Research Council 1999, 8, 86): "[T]o the extent that AVC [average variable

cost] mainly reflects the direct expenses incurred in production, it is an unsatisfactory proxy for marginal cost—since it does not account for more profitable opportunities forgone." By emphasizing revenue "self-diversion," the DOT was evidently attempting, correctly, to incorporate opportunity costs into its method of detecting predation (ibid. 1999, 166).

80. As I observed (Kahn 1991, 138):

> If I am right in characterizing the present trend of economic opinion on the subject, I suggest you might want to use as an example of the hog/corn cycle for your elementary economics classes the likelihood that the courts will for a very long time continue carrying the Chicago banners in the opposite direction, if anything with increasing unanimity—reflecting a decade of Reagan/Bush appointments and the very long time lag created by judicial life tenure.

In that same article, I suggested that the polling expert on the basis of whose findings a majority of the Supreme Court declared that "there is a consensus among commentators that predatory pricing schemes are rarely tried, and even more rarely successful," was probably a refugee from the *Literary Digest*—adding, parenthetically, "Those of you who do not grasp the historical allusion have the consolation of youth" (137).

81. There is reason, however, to be skeptical about the administrability of the particular—theoretically correct—test prescribed by the department's originally proposed rules. One can really envision the conflicting claims and offers of "proof" that the incumbents did or did not have available to them competitive responses more profitable than the ones they adopted. My own proposed resolution of this dilemma would be to leave the determination of what would be the least unprofitable response to competitive entry, absent a predatory intent, to the incumbent carriers themselves, by a simple requirement that if their response does indeed succeed in driving the challenger out, they be required to maintain those levels of capacity and fares for some substantial period of time—say, two years. That would tend to ensure that an incumbent carrier would not lightly undertake a profit-sacrificing (and therefore putatively predatory) response in the expectation of being able to withdraw it if it succeeds in driving out the challenger; and, at the same time, give travelers the continuing benefit of the newly introduced competition for some substantial period of time, rather than permit its quick withdrawal.

82. See Pitofsky (2000, 2).

83. Albert A. Foer (Foer 2000) of the American Antitrust Institute pointed out:

> [I]t has gradually become apparent that passage of the Hart-Scott-Rodino Act [requiring prior notification to the antitrust agencies of intentions to merge] in 1976 had the largely unanticipated effect of moving the merger process from a regime of post-hoc judicial review to preconsummation administrative negotiation. Relatively few merger cases are litigated.
>
> This is a negotiated process, with the agencies exercising the powerful lever of the threat of litigation and delay.

84. "SBC–Ameritech Merger Gets FCC Approval with Companies' 'Voluntary Commitments'," *Telecommunications Reports*, October 11, 1999.

85. The commission was evidently so pleased with its success in those negotiations that it elicited similar or identical commitments as the condition for its later approval of the Bell Atlantic–GTE merger (Federal Communications Commission 2000b).

86. See Federal Communications Commission (1999b, par. 363).

87. The act imposes that requirement only for the offer of newly authorized interLATA service and only for an initial three-year period.

88. See Federal Communications Commission (1999b, par. 376). According to the Furchtgott-Roth dissent, some of the "voluntary payments" by the parties for defaults on one or another commitment to facilitate competitive entry would be earmarked "to a fund to provide telecommunications services to underserved areas, groups, or persons" (ibid., attachment C, par. 59(5)d).

89. See ibid., par. 390.

90. See ibid., par. 391.

91. See ibid., par. 392.

92. See ibid., par. 400.

93. See ibid., par. 398.

94. Decrees in antitrust cases have, of course, frequently imposed obligations on offending parties to assist competitors positively—for example, by requiring licensing of their patents. But those have served as remedies to demonstrated (or, in the case of consent settlements, asserted) illegal monopolizations—not as prior conditions for the approval of putatively anticompetitive mergers.

95. See Federal Communications Commission (1999b, par. 187).

96. See ibid., 84, n. 344.

97. See p. 24, above.

98. See Federal Communications Commission (2000c and 1999e).

99. See Weisman (1999). See also Taylor (1994, 132–41), who found that reverse-traffic elasticity is "strong" and credited A. C. Larson, Dale E. Lehman, and Dennis L. Weisman with first incorporating it in a demand model.

100. See Federal Communications Commission (1999b), "Statement of Commissioner Michael K. Powell, Concurring in Part and Dissenting in Part," notes deleted.

101. It is perhaps unnecessary to make clear that I am not contending that the commission there exceeded its legal authority. It does have the responsibility of determining whether a merger in telecommunications is "in the public interest," and the commission's application of a "public interest, convenience, and necessity" (par. 354) test in "accepting"—or exacting—thirty conditions may have been legally no less appropriate than exaction by the antitrust agencies of conditions designed to forestall impairments of competition stemming from mergers. My central point is only that whereas the Civil Aeronautics Board, in the process of deregulation, defined the "public convenience and necessity" as consisting of the initiation of unregulated competition, the FCC has instead defined it as permitting the imposition of a complex of pervasive regulations, some of them with little and others with nothing to do with the way in which a deregulated market functions or would function.

102. See Kahn (1998, 86–87, especially n. 118).

103. In terms even of such a scale of preferences, the rule can be irrational: if the affiliate is free to buy or not buy from the utility affiliate, how does it serve the interests of *ratepayers* for the utility company to be forced to *try* to sell goods and services to the affiliate at *fully distributed* cost and fail, where that exceeds both incremental costs and market value, thereby losing sales that could make a net contribution, above incremental cost, to their benefit?

104. As of early 2001, there were 81 privately owned and more than 119 municipal electric utility companies involved in providing—or planning to provide—telecommunications services, typically using their existing rights of way, conduits, and fiber-optic facilities employed heretofore as part of their electric power distribution networks (*UT Digest Quarterly* 2001).

105. See, for example, Gordon and Olson (1999).

106. I am indebted to my colleague, Anne Selting, for clearly exposing that arithmetic to me.

107. This seems to be precisely the discount that the Telecommunications Act of 1996 requires the local telephone

companies to give to resellers of its retail services—discounts equated to the "costs that will be avoided" by the telephone company in making those sales at wholesale rather than retail (sec. 252(d)(3))—a clear prescription of efficient component pricing. I have bitterly criticized at length elsewhere (Kahn 1998, 96–99; Kahn, Tardiff, and Weisman 1999, 342–46) the FCC's interpretation of that instruction as authorizing it to require discounts equated to the hypothetical TSLRIC–BS of the entire retailing function—estimated by it as ranging between 17 and 25 percent—rather than the presumably much smaller LRIC that the local telephone company would actually save by selling some portion of its services at wholesale rather than retail (while almost certainly not abandoning the retailing function entirely)—an interpretation of the efficient component pricing rule explicitly endorsed by one of its original proponents: "It should be noted that the pertinent output increment for which the cost is calculated is the volume of business that is expected to be lost to competitors" (Baumol 1999).

The commission responded to similar complaints of the incumbent local telephone companies in its brief responding to their appeal before the Eighth Circuit Court. I make no effort to appraise its legal arguments in support of its interpretation of "costs that will be avoided"—the plain statutory language, which it characterizes as "ambiguous"—by, in effect, adding the phrase "if the ILEC gets out of retailing entirely," or its contention that that "interpretation of the wholesale rate standard . . . is reasonable and entitled to deference." Its supporting economic rationalization, however, requires a response.

If an ILEC were required to give resellers wholesale discounts equivalent only to the—presumably small amount of—costs that it saves in making those particular sales at wholesale, the FCC reasoning goes, the effect would be that "a portion of incumbents' *retailing* costs [would] be included in the *wholesale* price that new entrants have to pay, even though the new entrant is not causing those retail costs"; that such an interpretation of the act "would have the new entrants (which have their own retailing costs) subsidize the incumbents' retail offerings"; and that, instead, the only way to ensure efficient competition is "that the wholesale rate . . . is the same for everyone and leaves the market participants to compete . . . on the basis of their *retail* costs" (Federal Communications Commission 1999a, 75).

The corresponding responses are, first, that forcing an ILEC to offer resellers discounts greater than the costs it avoids by making those sales at wholesale forces *it* to subsidize *its competitors*. Second, the FCC's implicit premise is that the typical resellers will not themselves already be heavily involved in retailing telecommunications services, with the result that taking on the reselling of some ILEC local services will cause them to incur the (entire) TSLRIC of undertaking the retail function from scratch. But that is manifestly not true of the hundreds of sellers of long-distance services—facilities-based and resellers—who are or presumably would be seeking to add local exchange services to round out their existing offerings; or of the other, rapidly growing competitive local exchange carriers, employing their own facilities and the network elements provided them by the incumbent firms themselves.

As my reference to the act's prescription of efficient component pricing clearly implies, economic efficiency requires that competition be conducted on the basis of the respective actual LRICs of incumbents and challengers—reflecting such economies of scope as each may enjoy—not that entrants for whom that LRIC is the same as the TSLRIC of entering retailing from the ground up—because they enjoy no such economies and therefore are less efficient retailers in this respect—be subsidized by forcing the incumbents to give them discounts greater than the costs the former in fact avoid. Only if the reseller can provide the services in question at incremental costs equal to or lower than the costs that the ILEC actually saves by making them available for resale—taking into account also, as the market will, the value that those resold services add to its other offerings with which they may be packaged—will it deserve to survive.

To my considerable satisfaction, the Eighth Circuit Court of Appeals, in its decision of July 2000, agreed with the plaintiffs that the "clear language of the Statute" required them to offer wholesale discounts equal only to the costs they would actually avoid by making those sales rather than the hypothetical costs saved by abandoning retailing entirely.

With the exception of a recently mandated discount on broadband access to cable by Internet service providers, Canada has merely required that resellers have access to the retail rates or rate schedules of the incumbent phone companies, without any prescribed additional discount. In a proceeding under the New Zealand Commerce Act, I have testified on behalf on Telstra, a competitive entrant, in a suit against the dominant New Zealand

Telecom Company, in support only of a similar entitlement, without any prescribed discount—let alone one based on a TSLRIC–BS measure of avoided cost.

108. See, for example, Flaim (2000, 41–43). See also Joskow (2000a).

109. As Flaim pointed out (2000, 44–46, 53), this important competitive opportunity will be foreclosed so long as the regulated charge for default service continues to provide that protection; she therefore recommended that it cease to do so.

110. In view of Joskow's (2000a) demonstration that retail rates typically subsidize small residential users, by recovering a large share of fixed customer costs in variable energy charges, with the consequence that competition is likely in any event to concentrate on the larger, overcharged customers, it may be that shopping credits greater than avoided costs would merely redress that previous cross-subsidization. It would be entertaining to observe the reaction of populist advocates of such inflated credits, in the name of "competition," if one were to offer them that rationalization of their efforts.

111. I should perhaps take pleasure in that surreptitious or unconscious second-best method of reversing the previous cross-subsidization described in the preceding footnote. It would do so, however, only with the unfortunate income distributional consequences to which I have just alluded. In my experience, first-best beats second-best, whenever it is achievable to a reasonable approximation. See, for example, Kahn (1979, 3, 5, 7, 9–12).

References

AT&T Corp. 2000. *GTE Service Corp. et al. v. Federal Communications Commission et al.* Brief in the U.S. Supreme Court. No. 99-1244. September 28.

AT&T Corp. v. Iowa Utilities Board. 1999. 525 U.S. 366.

Areeda, Philip E. 1989. "Essential Facilities: An Epithet in Need of Limiting Principles." *Antitrust Law Journal* 58: 841, 852.

Baumol, William J. 1999. "Having Your Cake: How to Preserve Universal-Service Cross-Subsidies While Facilitating Competitive Entry." *Yale Journal on Regulation* 16: 1–17.

Baumol, William J., Paul L. Joskow, and Alfred E. Kahn. 1995. *The Challenge for Federal and State Regulators: Transition from Regulation to Efficient Competition in Electric Power.* Washington, D.C.: Edison Electric Institute.

Baumol, William J., Janusz A. Ordover, and Robert D. Willig. 1996. Comments of AT&T Corp. CC Docket 96-98: In the Matter of Implementation of Local Competition Provisions in the Telecommunications Act of 1996, appendix C. May 14; filed May 16.

Baumol, William J., John C. Panzar, and Robert D. Willig. 1982. *Contestable Markets and the Theory of Industry Structure.* San Diego: Harcourt Brace and Jovanovich.

Baumol, William J., and J. Gregory Sidak. 1995. *Transmission Pricing and Stranded Costs in the Electric Power Industry.* Washington, D.C.: AEI Press.

Bernheim, Douglas B., and Robert D. Willig. 1994. "An Analysis of the MFJ Line of Business Restrictions." Response on Behalf of AT&T to Motion of Bell Atlantic Corporation, BellSouth Corporation, NYNEX Corporation, and Southwestern Bell Corporation to Vacate the Decree. *United States v. Western Electric.* Civil Action No. 82-0192. December 1.

Bhagwat, Ashutosh. 1999. "Unnatural Competition? Applying the New Antitrust Learning to Foster Competition in the Local Exchange." *Hastings Law Journal* 50 (6): 1–23.

Coase, Ronald. 1937. "The Nature of the Firm." *Economica* 4: 386–405.

Costello, Kenneth W. 2000. "Do Codes of Conduct Achieve Their Objective?" *Electricity Journal* (March): 55–66.

Crandall, Robert W. 1999. "The Telecom Act's Phone-y Deregulation." *Wall Street Journal,* January 27.

———. 2000. "Local and Long Distance Competition: Replacing Regulation with Competition." In Jeffrey A. Eisenach and Randolph J. May, eds., *Communications Deregulation and FCC Reform: What Comes Next?* Washington, D.C.: Progress and Freedom Foundation, 39–58.

Crandall, Robert W., and Jerry A. Hausman. 2000. "Competition in U.S. Telecommunications Services: Effects of the 1996 Legislation." In Sam Pelzman and Clifford Winston, eds., *Deregulation of Network Industries: The Next Steps.* Washington D.C.: AEI–Brookings Joint Center for Regulatory Studies. 73–112.

Federal Communications Commission. 1996a. In the Matter of Implementation of the Local Competition Provisions in the Telecommunications Act of 1996. Notice of Proposed Rulemaking. CC Docket No. 96-98. Released April 19.

———. 1996b. In the Matter of Implementation of the Local Competition Provisions in the Telecommunications Act of 1996 (CC Docket No. 96-98) Interconnection between Local Exchange Carriers and Commercial Mobile Radio Service Providers (CC Docket No. 95-185). First Report and Order. Adopted August 1. Released August 8.

———. 1999a. Brief for Respondents. In the United States Court of Appeals for the Eighth Circuit, No. 96-3321 (and consolidated cases). *Iowa Utilities Board v. FCC.* August 16.

———. 1999b. In re Application of Ameritech Corp., Transferor, and SBC Communications Inc., Transferee, for Consent to Transfer Control of Corporations Holding Commission Licenses and Lines Pursuant to Sections 214 and 310(d) of the Communications Act and Parts 5, 22, 24, 25, 63, 90, 95 and 101 of the Commission's Rules. CC Docket No. 98-141. Adopted October 6. Released October 8.

———. 1999c. In the Matter of Federal-State Joint Board on Universal Service (CC Docket 96-45) and Forward-Looking Mechanism for High Cost Support for Non-Rural LECs (CC Docket No. 97-160), Tenth Report and Order (FCC 99-304). Adopted October 21. Released November 2.

————. 1999d. In the Matters of Application Deployment of Wireline Services Offering Advanced Telecommunications Capability and Implementation of the Local Competition Provisions of the Telecommunications Act of 1996. CC Docket Nos. 99-147 and 96-98. Adopted November 18. Released December 9.

————. 1999e. In the Matter of Application by Bell Atlantic New York for Authorization Under Section 271 of the Communications Act to Provide In-Region, InterLATA Service in the State of New York. Memorandum Opinion and Order. CC Docket No. 99-295. Adopted December 21. Released December 22.

————. 2000a. *Telecommunications @ the Millennium: The Telecom Act Turns Four.* Washington, D.C.: Federal Communications Commission, Office of Plans and Policy. February 8.

————. 2000b. In re Application of GTE Corporation, Transferor, and Bell Atlantic Corporation, Transferee, for Consent to Transfer Control of Domestic and International Sections 214 and 310 Authorizations and Application to Transfer Control of a Submarine Cable Landing License. CC Docket No. 98-184. Adopted June 16. Released June 16.

————. 2000c. Memorandum Opinion and Order in the Matter of Application of SBC Communications Inc., Southwestern Bell Telephone Company, and Southwestern Bell Communications Services, Inc. d/b/a Southwestern Bell Long Distance Pursuant to Section 271 of the Telecommunications Act of 1996 to Provide in-Region, InterLATA Services in Texas. CC Docket No. 00-65. Adopted June 30. Released June 30.

————. 2000d. Brief for the Federal Communications Commission and the United States, In the Supreme Court of the United States, No. 99-1244, *GTE Service Corporation et al., Petitioners v. Federal Communications Commission and the United States of America.* September 2000.

Federal Energy Regulatory Commission. 1996. Order No. 888, 18CFR Part 35 and 385. Docket Nos. RM 95-98 and 94-97. April 24.

Fellner, William J. 1958. "The Influence of Market Structure on Technological Progress." In American Economic Association, *Readings in Industrial Organization and Public Policy* (Homewood, Ill.: Richard D. Irwin).

Flaim, Theresa. 2000. "The Big Retail 'Bust': What Will It Take to Get True Competition?" *Electricity Journal* 13 (3): 41–54.

Foer, Albert A. 2000. Draft 2-22-00 of essay for FTC:WATCH, "Bringing Restructuring Out of the Closet," received in an e-mail dated February 22 (no pagination).

Gordon, Kenneth, and Wayne P. Olson. 1999. "Getting It Right: Filling the Gaps in FERC's Stranded Cost Policies." *Electricity Journal* 12 (4): 69–79.

Grimm, Curtis, and Clifford Winston. 2000. "Competition in the Deregulated Railroad Industry: Sources, Effects, and Policy Issues." In Sam Pelzman and Clifford Winston, eds., *Deregulation of Network Industries: The Next Steps.* Washington, D.C.: AEI–Brookings Joint Center for Regulatory Studies. 41–71.

Hahn, Robert W. 1999. "Let the Market Control Faster Access to the Internet." AEI–Brookings Joint Center for Regulatory Studies *Policy Matter* 99-8. December.

Hausman, Jerry A., and J. Gregory Sidak. 1999. "A Consumer-Welfare Approach to the Mandatory Unbundling of Telecommunications Networks." *Yale Law Journal* 109: 417–505.

Hazlett, Thomas W. 1999. "Economic and Political Consequences of the 1996 Telecommunications Act." AEI–Brookings Joint Center Working Paper 99-8. September.

Hurdle, Gloria, Richard Johnson, Andrew S. Joskow, Gregory J. Werden, and Michael A. Williams. 1989. "Concentration, Potential Entry, and Performance in the Airline Industry." *Journal of Industrial Economics* 38 (2): 119–39.

Iowa Utilities Board et al. v. Federal Communications Commission, 219 F. 3d 744 (2000).

Janisch, Hudson N. 1998. "So Near and Yet So Far: A Comparative Analysis of Network Unbundling and Local Competition." Paper prepared for the Twenty-sixth Telecommunications Policy Research Conference. October 3.

Joskow, Paul L. 2000a. "Why Do We Need Electricity Retailers? or Can You Get It Cheaper Wholesale?" Unpublished discussion draft. Sloan School of Management and Center for Energy and Environmental Policy Research at MIT. February 13 version cited.

———. 2000b. "Deregulation and Regulatory Reform in the U.S. Electric Power Sector." In Sam Pelzman and Clifford Winston, eds., *Deregulation of Network Industries: The Next Steps.* Washington, D.C.: AEI–Brookings Joint Center for Regulatory Studies. 113–88.

Kahn, Alfred E. 1970 and 1971. *The Economics of Regulation,* vols. 1 and 2. New York: John Wiley. Reprinted by MIT Press, 1988, with a new "Introduction: A Postscript, Seventeen Years After."

———. 1974. "Economic Theory as a Guideline for Government Intervention and Control: Comment." *Journal of Economic Issues* 8 (2) 301–7.

———. 1975. "Between Theory and Practice: Reflections of a Neophyte Public Utility Regulator." *Public Utilities Fortnightly.* January 2. 3–7.

———. 1979. "Applications of Economics to an Imperfect World." Richard T. Ely Lecture. *American Economic Review, Papers and Proceedings* 69 (2):1–3.

———. 1982. "The Political Feasibility of Regulatory Reform: How Did We Do It?" In Leroy Graymer and Frederick Thompson, eds., *Reforming Social Regulation: Alternative Public Policy Strategies.* Beverly Hills, Calif.: Sage Publications.

———. 1983. "Deregulation and Vested Interests: The Case of Airlines." In Roger G. Noll and Bruce M. Owen, eds., *The Political Economy of Deregulation.* Washington, D.C.: American Enterprise Institute.

———. 1984a. "The Road to More Intelligent Telephone Pricing." *Yale Journal on Regulation* 1 (2): 139–57.

———. 1984b. "The Uneasy Marriage of Regulation and Competition." *Telematics.* September. 1–2, 8–17.

———. 1985. "Who Should Pay for Power-Plant Duds?" *Wall Street Journal.* August 15.

———. 1991. "Thinking about Predation—A Personal Diary." *Review of Industrial Organization* 6: 137–46.

———. 1995. "Incremental Cost Standards for Network Unbundling." Paper submitted to the Connecticut Department of Public Utility Control, Docket Nos. 94-10-01-02, on behalf of the Southern New England Telephone Company. January 10.

———. 1996a. "Thirteen Steps to Reconciliation." *Regulation*, no. 4. 14–16.

———. 1996b. "How to Treat the Costs of Shared Voice and Video Networks in a Postregulatory Age." Cato Institute *Policy Analysis* no. 264. November 27.

———. 1996c. Cerified Statement before the Surface Transportation Board on Behalf of the National Industrial Transportation League and the Western Coal Traffic League Commenting on the Joint Statement Submitted by the Association of American Railroads. Docket No. 41626, Docket No. 41242, Docket No. 41295. November 27.

———. 1997. "Competition and Stranded Costs Re-Revisited." *Natural Resources Journal* 37 (1): 29–42.

———. 1998. *Letting Go: Deregulating the Process of Deregulation.* East Lansing: Michigan State University Institute of Public Utilities. July.

———. 1999a. "Comments on Exclusionary Airline Pricing." *Journal of Air Transport Management* 5 (1): 1–12.

———. 1999b. "Declaration of Alfred E. Kahn in Response to Second Further Notice of Proposed Rulemaking." Before the Federal

Communications Commission. In the Matter of Implementation of the Local Competition Provisions in the Telecommunications Act of 1996. Testimony submitted on behalf of GTE–Bell Atlantic. CC Docket No. 96-98. May 26.

———. 1999c. "Reply Declaration of Alfred E. Kahn in Response to Second Further Notice of Proposed Rulemaking." Before the Federal Communications Commission. In the Matter of Implementation of the Local Competition Provisions in the Telecommunications Act of 1996. CC Docket No. 96-98. June 10.

Kahn, Alfred E., and William Shew. 1987. "Current Issues in Telecommunications Regulation: Pricing." *Yale Journal on Regulation* 4 (spring): 191–256.

Kahn, Alfred E., Timothy J. Tardiff, and Dennis L. Weisman. 1999. "The Telecommunications Act at Three Years: An Economic Evaluation of Its Implementation by the Federal Communications Commission." *Information Economics and Policy* (December): 319–65.

Kearney, Joseph D., and Thomas W. Merrill. 1998. "The Great Transformation of Regulated Industries Law." *Columbia Law Review* 98: 1323–409.

Lehman, Dale E., and Dennis L. Weisman. 2000. "The Political Economy of Price-Cap Regulation." *Review of Industrial Organization* 16: 343–56.

Lipsky, Abbott B., Jr., and J. Gregory Sidak. 1999. "Essential Facilities." *Stanford Law Review* 51 (5): 1187–248.

Litan, Robert E., and Roger G. Noll. 1998. "Unleashing Telecommunications: The Case for True Competition." Brookings Institution *Policy Brief* no. 39. November.

Lyon, Leverett S., and Victor Abramson. 1940. *Government and Economic Life: Development and Current Issues of American Public Policy,* vol. 2. Washington, D.C.: Brookings Institution.

Madison Gas & Electric. 1974. Wisconsin Public Service Commission Decision. August 8.

Morrison, Steven A., and Clifford Winston. 1987. "Empirical Implications and Tests of the Contestability Hypothesis." *Journal of Law and Economics* 30 (April): 53–66.

———. 1995. *The Evolution of the Airline Industry.* Washington, D.C.: Brookings Institution Press.

———. 2000. "The Remaining Role for Government Policy in the Deregulated Airline Industry." In Sam Pelzman and Clifford Winston, eds., *Deregulation of Network Industries: The Next Steps.* Washington, D.C.: AEI–Brookings Joint Center for Regulatory Studies. 1–40.

Noll, Roger G. 1999. *The Economics and Politics of the Slowdown in Regulatory Reform.* Washington, D.C.: AEI–Brookings Joint Center for Regulatory Studies.

Noll, Roger G., and Bruce M. Owen, eds. 1983. *The Political Economy of Deregulation.* Washington, D.C.: American Enterprise Institute.

Pitofsky, Robert. 2000. "The Nature and Limits of Restructuring and Merger Review." Remarks at the Cutting Edge Antitrust Conference. Law Seminars International. February 7.

Schwartz, Marius. 1997. Affidavit of Professor Marius Schwartz, filed on behalf of the Department of Justice in response to Southwestern Bell's Oklahoma petition. CC Docket No. 97-121. May 14.

———. 2000. "The Economic Logic for Conditioning Bell Entry into Long Distance on the Prior Opening of Local Markets." AEI–Brookings Joint Center for Regulatory Studies Working Paper 00-4. April.

Tardiff, Timothy J. 1999. "The Forecasting Implications of Telecommunications Cost Models." In James Alleman and Eli Noam, eds., *The New Investment Theory of Real Options and Its Implications for Telecommunications Economics.* Boston: Kluwer Academic Publishers. 181–90.

Taylor, Lester D. 1994. *Telecommunications Demand in Theory and Practice.* Boston: Kluwer Academic Publishers.

Thierer, Adam D. 1999. *Broadband Telecommunications in the 21st Century: Five Principles for Reform.* Heritage Foundation *Backgrounder* no. 1317. September 2.

Transportation Research Board/National Research Council. 1999. "Entry and Competition in the U.S. Airline Industry, Issues and Opportunities." Special Report 255. Washington, D.C.

U.S. Department of Transportation. 1998. Statement of Enforcement Policy Regarding Unfair Exclusionary Conduct. Notice 98-16. April. Reproduced in Transportation Research Board/National Research Council (1999): 159–85.

United States v. Aluminum Co. of America. 1945. 148 F. 2d. 416.

UT Digest Quarterly. 2001. April.

Warren-Boulton, Frederick R. 1998. Direct Testimony on Behalf of AT&T Communications of the Southwest, Inc., and MCI Telecommunications. Kansas State Corporation Commission. Docket No. 97-SWBT-411-GIT. May 12.

Weisman, Dennis L. 1994. "Why Less May Be More under Price-Cap Regulation." *Journal of Regulatory Economics* 6: 339–62.

———. 1999. "Footprints in Cyberspace: Toward a Theory of Mergers in Network Industries." *Info.* August. 367–69.

———. 1997. Direct Testimony on Behalf of Southwestern Bell before the Texas Public Utilities Commission. Docket 16189 et al. September 15. 4, 9–10.

Williamson, Oliver E. 1979. "Transaction-Cost Economics: The Governance of Contractual Relations." *Journal of Law and Economics* 22: 233–61.

Winston, Clifford. 1998. "U.S. Industry Adjustment to Economic Deregulation." *Journal of Economic Perspectives* 12 (3): 89–110.

About the Author

Alfred E. Kahn is the Robert Julius Thorne Professor of Political Economy at Cornell University. He has held the Thorne chair since 1967 and was dean of Cornell's College of Arts and Sciences from 1969 to 1974. From 1974 to 1977 Professor Kahn served as chairman of the New York Public Service Commission. In 1977 President Jimmy Carter appointed him chairman of the Civil Aeronautics Board, and in October 1978, after he had engineered the sunsetting of the CAB, President Carter appointed him Adviser to the President on Inflation and chairman of the Council on Wage and Price Stability, in which post he was known as the "inflation czar."

In addition to *The Economics of Regulation* (John Wiley, 1970 and 1971; reprinted by MIT Press in 1988) and this volume, Professor Kahn's books have included *Letting Go: Deregulating the Process of Deregulation* (Michigan State University Institute of Public Utilities, 1998), *Integration and Competition in the Petroleum Industry*, Petroleum Monograph Series, vol. 3 (Yale University Press, 1959; reprinted in 1971) (with Melvin G. DeChazeau), *Fair Competition, The Law and Economics of Antitrust Policy* (Cornell University Press, 1954; reprinted by Greenwood Press in 1970) (with Joel B. Dirlam), and *Great Britain in the World Economy* (Columbia University Press, 1946; reprinted in 1968). Professor Kahn is also the author of numerous scholarly articles and advisory commission reports and has testified before state, federal, and international courts and commissions.

The recipient of Yale University's Wilbur Cross Medal for Outstanding Achievement (1995), the L. Welch Pogue Award for Lifetime Contributions to Aviation (1997), the Sovereign Fund Award (1997), the New York University Distinguished Alumni Award (1976), and the J. Rhoads Foster Award (1999), Professor Kahn is a member of the American Academy of Arts and Sciences and the American Economic Association (vice president, 1981–1982) and was a member of the first National Economic Advisory Council to the American Telephone & Telegraph Company. He has also been a member of the usage panel of *The American Heritage Dictionary* since 1982.

JOINT CENTER